Four Women of Courage

Four Women of Courage

Edited, with commentary by Bennett Wayne

GARRARD PUBLISHING COMPANY
CHAMPAIGN, ILLINOIS

Picture credits:

American Foundation for the Blind: p. 94
The Bettmann Archive: pp. 18, 29, 54, 61, 65, 70, 78
Brown Brothers: pp. 37, 105, 109, 126, 144 (bottom left), 159 (bottom)
Jacqueline Cochran: p. 151
Culver Pictures: pp. 47, 83, 88, 117, 144 (bottom right), 163
Bill Ray, Time—LIFE Picture Agency: p. 6
Reminiscences of America's First Trained Nurse by Linda Richards.
   Courtesy of New Rochelle Hospital School of Nursing,
   New Rochelle, N.Y.: pp. 41, 75
Trenton Psychiatric Hospital: pp. 9, 32
Wide World Photos: pp. 100, 114, 133, 144 (top), 145, 154 (both),
   159 (top)

Library of Congress Cataloging in Publication Data

Wayne, Bennett.
   Four women of courage.

   (Target books)
  SUMMARY: Brief biographies of four women who achieved their ambitions against great odds.
   1. Cochran, Jacqueline—Juvenile literature.
2. Dix, Dorothea Lynde, 1802–1887—Juvenile literature.
3. Keller, Helen Adams, 1880–1968—Juvenile literature.
4. Richards, Melinda Ann Judson, 1841–1930—Juvenile literature. [1. Cochran, Jacqueline. 2. Dix, Dorothea Lynde, 1802–1887. 3. Keller, Helen Adams, 1880–1968. 4. Richards, Melinda Ann Judson, 1841–1930. 5. Women—Biography] I. Title.
HQ1412.W39   920.72 [920]   74–13482
ISBN 0–8116–4911–3

Copyright © 1975 by Garrard Publishing Company
All rights reserved. Manufactured in the U.S.A.

Contents

True Grit 7
DOROTHEA DIX: Crusader for Mental Hospitals 9
LINDA RICHARDS: First American Trained Nurse 41
HELEN KELLER: Toward the Light 83
JACQUELINE COCHRAN: First Lady of Flight 117
Index 165

True Grit

This woman firefighter and others like her face danger every day of their lives. Their bravery makes headlines, but there are other kinds of courage too: the quiet determination to face personal handicaps and overcome them, the firm resolve to fight for a worthy cause even though it is unpopular. Over the years, in every walk of life, women have been famous both for their daring and their determination. They had true grit!

This book is about four women who lived at different times and whose lives followed different paths. They had one great thing in common—courage in its many forms. Flyer Jacqueline Cochran overcame an unhappy childhood and went on to prove her physical courage in a man's world. Helen Keller was a fighter too, but she fought a quiet battle against her own handicaps. Both blind and deaf, she overcame her disabilities and went on to help others with similar problems. Dorothea Dix had pluck. She refused to take no for an answer in her struggle to provide better care for the mentally ill. Against great odds, Linda Richards opened doors for women in medicine when she became America's first trained nurse.

Each of these women had a different goal, but each one set about reaching it in the same way—with courage.

DOROTHEA DIX
1802–1887

Dorothea Dix began her life's work by accident. In the dark dungeon of a jail she was visiting, Dorothea found mentally ill people caged, chained, and beaten like animals. It horrified her. Although she was not well herself, this tiny woman started a revolution that completely changed care for the insane. Hers was a rare kind of courage. It was courage to fight for an unpopular cause and to keep on fighting even when things looked hopeless. It was the kind of courage that turns defeat into victory. Before Dorothea Dix there was disease, filth, and suffering for mental patients. After her there was kinder treatment, thirty new and better hospitals, and hope for those who had been forgotten.

Dorothea Dix
Crusader for Mental Hospitals

by Mary Malone

Copyright © 1968
by Mary Malone

1. Orange Court

Seven-year-old Dorothea Dix walked about the garden at Orange Court, smelling the lovely spring flowers. She always felt happy here at her grandparents' home in Boston.

Suddenly she stopped. Her grandfather, Dr. Elijah Dix, hurried from the big, red-brick house. His carriage was waiting in the driveway.

Dorothea ran over to him. "Grandfather, may I go with you?"

His eyes twinkled. "Is that why you are all dressed up, Dolly?"

She shook her head. "No. Grandmother said my old clothes were ragged."

Every time Dorothea came to Orange Court, the same thing happened. A maid scrubbed her and helped her put on new clothes. Then Dorothea went to her grandmother. "Now," grandmother said, "you look like my namesake."

Grandfather Dix was rich and successful. But his son, Dorothea's father, was a failure. At nineteen, Joseph Dix had left Harvard College to get married.

Then he and his wife moved from Boston to southern Maine. They lived in a little village called Hampden.

Dorothea was born in 1802 in a one-room, tumble-down cottage. Four years later her brother Joseph was born, and then Charles. Mr. Dix was nervous and moody. He seldom kept a job for long.

The family would have been hungry if grandfather had not helped. Mrs. Dix was sickly and was always complaining about her health. Neither she nor Mr. Dix showed much love for their children. Dorothea was the one who really looked after the little boys.

Sometimes Dr. Dix came to see them and took Dorothea to Boston for a visit. At Orange Court she had a room of her own and time to play. Best of all, she had grandfather. No matter how busy he was, he always found time for her. He had taught her to read from the books in his library.

Now she slipped her hand in his. "Please take me with you."

Dr. Dix nodded. "I will, if you won't get tired. I have a great many patients to visit."

One afternoon they were on the way home. "You will have to go back to Hampden tomorrow, Dolly," he said. "Your mother has sent for you."

"Oh, grandfather!" she cried. "Why can't I live with you?"

"I wish you could, Dolly. But your grandmother

says she is too old to start raising another family. If we were to keep you here, we'd have to send for your brothers too. They could not get along in Hampden without you."

"But I would look after them here," Dorothea said. "I'll tell grandmother that."

Soon grandfather's carriage stopped in front of Orange Court. Dorothea went to look for grandmother. She opened the parlor door without knocking.

Grandmother was having tea with her sister, Sarah Duncan.

Madam Dix, as the doctor's wife was known in Boston, looked up. "Dorothea! Where are your manners?"

"I'm sorry, grandmother," Dorothea began, "but. . . ."

"You must learn better," grandmother said. "Please go to your room."

Unhappily, the girl went upstairs. She had lost her chance to ask about staying at Orange Court.

2. Home in Hampden

The next morning grandfather put Dorothea on the stagecoach for Hampden. No one met her there. She walked all alone in the rain, down a muddy lane to her home.

Her three-year-old brother Joseph was playing outside the Dix cottage. "Dolly!" he cried happily running to meet her.

Dorothea hugged him hard. Then she hurried inside to see the baby. Little Charles, too, smiled happily when he saw his sister.

"Is that you, Dorothea?" Her mother's voice came from a bed in a dim corner of the room.

"Yes, mother. I'm back."

Mrs. Dix sighed. "You'll have to feed the little ones. I'm too tired."

She did not ask about Dorothea's visit.

Dorothea's father was not home. Joseph Dix had failed at farming and selling books. Now he had become a preacher. He was doing better, but he was away for days at a time. He had to ride miles into the backwoods where there were no regular ministers.

He was away when a letter from Boston came for him several weeks later. When he returned, Dorothea gave him the letter. She waited expectantly for the news from Orange Court.

Her father's face told her that something was wrong. "My father is dead," he said, turning away.

Dorothea's eyes filled with tears. "I will never see grandfather again!" she sobbed.

As she grew older, life became even harder for Dorothea. Her happiness at Orange Court was only a memory. At Hampden she did most of the work.

She hauled water, built the fires, and weeded the garden. She also helped her father with his work. He had copies of his sermons printed. Dorothea sewed the pages together so he could sell them.

She taught her brothers to read and write, as Grandfather Dix had taught her. She wished she could go to school so that she could learn more.

"Mother, may I go to school this year?" she asked every fall when school opened.

"Girls should stay home," Mrs. Dix said.

When she was twelve, Dorothea decided to leave Hampden. She told her brothers first.

"I am going to Boston, to live with grandmother," she said. "She will let me go to school."

Little Charles began to cry. "Don't go, Dolly! Who will take care of me?"

Dorothea put her arms around him. "Mother and Joseph will manage," she said. "And I will send for you as soon as I can."

"Are you sure grandmother will take you?" Joseph asked.

"Of course," Dorothea said confidently. To herself, she added, "She must."

"But what will father say?" Joseph continued.

"If he says no, I'll run away!" she declared.

Dorothea's father did not want her to leave. However, she asked so often that finally he let her go.

3. From Boston to Worcester

Madam Dix was glad to see her granddaughter, for she had been lonely since Dr. Dix died. She nodded when Dorothea told her about leaving home. "Yes, it is time you learned how to be a lady. You are a Dix and you should plan to make a good marriage, just as I did."

"But I would like to go to school, grandmother," Dorothea said.

"Of course," grandmother said.

She sent Dorothea to the best school in Boston. The girl became a very good student. She enjoyed books and learning.

However, she did not like the household tasks that grandmother gave her.

"Learning to sew and to cook are part of your education," Madam Dix said.

Dorothea did not think so. She was careless about her clothes and was often late for meals.

Madam Dix scolded her.

Dorothea cried. She thought that she would never please her grandmother.

Before long Madam Dix decided that she needed help. She asked her sister Sarah and Sarah's daughter, Mrs. Sarah Fiske, for advice. "Maybe I am too old to train the girl," she said.

They were very understanding. "Let Dorothea come to us in Worcester for a few years," they said.

Mrs. Fiske added, "I will treat her like my own daughter."

Madam Dix decided to send Dorothea to Worcester. Dorothea's many relatives greeted her warmly. "My, how pretty you are," Mrs. Fiske said. This pleased Dorothea. Nobody had ever called her pretty before.

The two ladies were kind and patient. Soon Dorothea settled down. By the time she was fourteen, she could sew and cook almost as well as her cousin. "Your grandmother will be pleased with you, Dorothea," Mrs. Fiske said.

Dorothea had fun too. She had many cousins in Worcester, and they were all kind to her. She went walking and skating often with the girls.

One family of cousins, the Wheelers, invited her to visit them every Sunday afternoon. Their two little daughters, Nancy and Frances, liked Dorothea at once. "Tell us a story, Cousin Dolly," they begged.

One day as she talked to them, she heard someone say, "You are a born teacher."

She looked up to see a tall, fair-haired young man standing before her.

"Cousin Edward!" Nancy exclaimed.

Dorothea knew this must be her cousin, Edward Bangs. He was the son of Judge Bangs. Edward, a lawyer, had just returned from a trip south. At 28, he seemed very grown-up to Dorothea.

"So this is Dorothea Lynde Dix," he said, smiling. He seemed interested in her and asked questions about Boston. When he left, little Frances said, "Isn't he handsome, Cousin Dolly?" Dorothea agreed.

She saw Edward Bangs often after that. He began to meet her on Sunday afternoons as she walked to the Wheelers. They became good friends. Dorothea's other cousins began to tease her about her "beau."

4. First School

Telling stories to her young cousins gave Dorothea an idea. She would start a school. In those days, teachers were often very young.

Mrs. Fiske protested. "But you don't have to teach. Your grandfather left money for you. You will have it when you are 21."

"That is too long to wait!" Dorothea said. "I need money now so I can send for my brothers. They must have a better life. My parents will let them come."

Mrs. Fiske nodded. "The boys can live with us."

"Oh, thank you!" Dorothea exclaimed. "But what about my school, Cousin Sarah? May I start one?"

Mrs. Fiske smiled. "We will speak to Judge Bangs."

Dorothea had to wait until her cousins approved of

A one-room schoolhouse in the 1800s. Dorothea's first school looked much like this one.

her plan. Finally, they did. Edward Bangs rented an empty store on Main Street for the school.

The first day, Dorothea waited nervously for pupils to come. She had pinned up her hair and lengthened her skirts. She would be very strict. Then her pupils would not guess she was only fourteen.

"Good morning, Miss Dix!" Two little boys had popped their heads in the doorway, grinning.

Miss Dix! It had a grown-up sound. She knew the boys. "William and Levi Lincoln, you may sit in the first row."

Frances and Nancy Wheeler came next, then Joseph Eaton, Anne Bancroft, and Lucy Green. The very best families in Worcester were sending their children to Dorothea's school. When her brothers arrived, they were pupils too.

Dorothea taught the children reading, writing, and manners. Each one had to learn a chapter from the Bible every week and say it on Monday morning.

Miss Dix was firm but fair. She punished the children when they were naughty—and she was especially strict with her own brothers.

Dorothea loved teaching. She kept her school until she was seventeen. Then her grandmother sent for her, and she returned to Boston. Her brothers stayed in Worcester with Sarah Fiske. Later, they too went to Boston to live with Madam Dix and go to school.

5. A Busy Life

Madam Dix was pleased when she saw how attractive Dorothea had become.

"It is time for you to think about marriage," Madam Dix told her.

Dorothea knew that Edward Bangs was in love with her. She had promised to write to him and let him visit her in Boston. But she was not ready for marriage. There was so much she wanted to learn first.

In those days, women did not go to college. So Dorothea read books in the public library.

She learned about the famous preacher, Dr. William Channing. One Sunday, she went to his church to hear him. His goodness and kindness showed in every word he spoke. "The poor and the handicapped need our help," he said.

Dorothea kept going to hear Dr. Channing. One Sunday after the service, a pretty, dark-haired girl came up to her.

"We should know each other," the girl said. "I have seen you here often. I am Ann Heath, from Brookline."

Dorothea smiled. She liked the girl's friendliness. "I am Dorothea Lynde Dix."

"Isn't Dr. Channing wonderful?" Ann said.

"Oh, yes!" Dorothea replied. "If only I could do as he says and help others."

"I am sure you will," Ann said. "As for me, I must stay home and look after my family. Won't you come and visit?"

"I would love to," Dorothea said.

She and Ann became good friends. Dorothea liked the large, lively Heath family. "I always hate to leave your house," she told Ann.

After a few years Dorothea was ready to start teaching again. She asked her grandmother if she could have a girls' school in Orange Court.

Madam Dix did not like the idea of a school in her own house. "What will happen to my carpets and my furniture?" she cried.

But as usual, Dorothea had her way. She opened a second school, too, for poor children. This school was held every morning in the carriage house. Besides the schools, Dorothea managed the household for her grandmother. She also kept on with her own studies.

When her father died, she worked even harder to forget the sadness of her childhood. She saw that her mother was taken care of in a nursing home. Her brother Charles went to sea and became a sailor. Joseph went into business.

Dorothea's schools ran like clockwork. There was a time for everything. The girls especially loved the nature walks Miss Dix took with them almost every afternoon.

She wrote a book, based on her nature talks. She called it *Conversations on Common Things*. The book became very popular. Then she went on to write other tales and poems for children.

Dorothea's life was so full that she could not think of marriage. Edward Bangs grew tired of waiting for her. He married someone else.

At first Dorothea was upset. She would not talk about Edward, and she destroyed all of his letters. Later, she realized that her work and her friends brought her true happiness.

Dorothea and Ann Heath got to know Dr. Channing well. They visited him and his family in their Boston home. Dr. Channing became interested in Dorothea's work, especially her schools.

"But you are working too hard," he said. "You will ruin your health."

Dorothea admitted that she had a pain in her chest.

"Come with us to the seashore for the summer," Dr. Channing said. "You can be our children's governess and have a chance to rest too."

Dorothea was delighted. Later the Channings asked her to go with them to an island in the Caribbean. They spent six months there. Dorothea rested and became well.

When she returned to Boston, she worked just as hard as before. In a few years she was sick again.

"You have lung trouble," her doctor told her. "You must stop teaching and go to a warmer place to live."

Dr. Channing came to see her and agreed. "Go to Italy for the winter," he said. "But first, stop in England and visit my friends the Rathbones."

Dorothea was sorry she had to close her schools. But she had always wanted to travel abroad. She was glad when Madam Dix encouraged her to go on a long trip.

6. New Ideas

Dorothea's ship sailed for Europe in April 1836. The Atlantic was stormy. Most of the passengers were seasick. After six weeks they landed in Liverpool, England. Dorothea was so weak that she had to go to bed in her hotel.

The next morning, Dr. Channing's friends, the Rathbones, came to the hotel to see her. She was very ill.

"You are coming home to Greenbank with us," said kind Mrs. Rathbone. "You need care and rest."

"But you do not even know me," Dorothea whispered.

"It is enough for us that you are Dr. Channing's friend," Mr. Rathbone said.

Dorothea expected to stay only a short time with

her new friends. She never dreamed it would be eighteen months before she was well enough to leave. All that time the Rathbones looked after her. They were the kindest people Dorothea had ever known.

Mr. Rathbone was a rich merchant. He spent a great deal of time and money helping others. Many friends came to visit him at Greenbank.

One of the visitors Dorothea liked best was a gentle Quaker named Samuel Tuke. He was the doctor in charge of York Retreat, a home for insane people. In those days, mentally ill people were called "insane."

"The insane must be treated as sick people," Dr. Tuke said, "not as criminals or wild animals." He explained that in ancient times people thought insanity was caused by evil spirits. Later insane persons were shut away, sometimes in dungeons.

"Now," Dr. Tuke said, "there are a few hospitals that treat insanity as an illness. But only the rich can afford these hospitals. The poor are kept in jails and workhouses. Most of the time they are forgotten."

His angry eyes blazed as he went on. "Mental illness can be cured! We must make people see that it is an illness, not a crime."

Dorothea began to be excited by Dr. Tuke's ideas.

Bad news, however, came from home. First her mother died. Before Dorothea was well enough to travel, word came that Madam Dix had died too.

Sadly Dorothea wrote to Ann Heath, "There is no need to hurry home now."

She stayed at Greenbank until she was entirely well. Then in the fall of 1837, she said good-bye to her English friends.

"You have given me back my health," she told them. "I will never forget you."

The Rathbones had given her something else too—an interest in people who needed help. Now she was certain that she wanted to spend the rest of her life helping others.

7. Life Work

When Dorothea returned to Boston, some of her cousins were cool to her. They thought she should have been with Madam Dix during her last illness. Dorothea was hurt—and lonely. Orange Court was closed, so she lived in a boardinghouse. Her health would not allow her to teach. She was 36. It seemed as though the best years of her life were over.

She visited orphan homes and wrote more stories for children. But she was not satisfied.

She was looking for a "cause." She wanted a job that would take all of her time and skill. She found it on a rainy day in 1841.

A young man named John Nichols came to see her

at her boardinghouse. "I hope you can help me, Miss Dix," he said.

John Nichols was studying to be a minister. He was looking for a Sunday school teacher for the women prisoners in the East Cambridge Jail.

"It is not a pleasant place," he said. "Many women would be afraid. Could you suggest someone, Miss Dix?"

Dorothea nodded. "Yes. I can surely suggest someone—myself."

"Oh! But I have heard that you are in poor health," Mr. Nichols said.

"I shall be there next Sunday," Dorothea said firmly.

The following Sunday she faced a roomful of ragged women prisoners. She spoke softly and read to them in her low, beautiful voice. The restless women became quiet. Dorothea told them she would come back the next week.

Before she left she walked through the jail. There was one door the jailer would not open. "That's where insane people are kept," he said.

"I would like to see them."

"Why, ma'am, you couldn't stand it!"

"Please open the door," Dorothea insisted.

"Well, don't say I didn't warn you," the jailer grumbled. He unlocked the door.

Dorothea walked into a room that was bitterly cold

and damp. The air was bad. The noise made her want to cover her ears. Several women in rags huddled together for warmth. A few sobbed and cried. Dorothea walked around and spoke to them. She held their hands. Her heart was touched by the sad sight.

"These poor creatures will never get well here," she told the jailer.

"The insane don't get well," he said.

"At least give them a little heat," she continued.

He shook his head. "They don't feel the cold."

Dorothea decided something must be done. She went to the town council. The men on the council did not want to hear about the insane people in the jail. They even said she was a busybody.

"What shall I do?" she asked Dr. Channing.

"I am sure that Dr. Samuel Howe and Charles Sumner will help you," he said. "You must go to them."

Both of these famous men listened to Dorothea. Then they visited the jail and saw that she had spoken the truth. They wrote to the newspapers. They got people interested in conditions in the jail. At last, the town council did something. They provided heat for the insane people.

It was a small victory but it was important. It started Dorothea on her life work for the mentally ill.

Before, no one had spoken up for these poor forgotten people in public institutions. Now Dorothea

Lynde Dix had. She would work the rest of her life to improve the care and treatment of the mentally ill.

8. Famous Woman

For two years, Dorothea visited the jails in Massachusetts. She found some mentally ill people in every jail. They were treated far worse than criminals.

She wrote a report of what she had seen. She sent it to the state legislature where the laws were made. She knew now that the best way to work for her cause was through the state government.

In the report, Dorothea told about the mentally ill people she had seen locked in cages, closets, and pens. She had seen them chained and beaten.

The report was made public. It was like a bombshell exploding. People became angry, but for different reasons. Some people were angry because the state let such things happen. Many more were angry because they thought the report was not true.

Dorothea's friends, however, believed it. Dr. Channing, Dr. Howe, and the well-known educator, Horace Mann, all encouraged her. They helped to get a law passed to make the State Hospital at Worcester bigger. All mentally ill people in the state could go there.

This was Dorothea's first big success.

In the mid-1800s the mentally ill were treated more like criminals than like sick people.

She went on to Connecticut and Rhode Island. She found the same kinds of conditions there. In Rhode Island she found an insane man chained in a stone cell. The room had no light or fresh air. She asked some of the rich people in the state to give money for a hospital for the insane. A man named Cyrus Butler was on her list.

"He is a hard man to part from his money," friends told her.

In Mr. Butler's office, Dorothea went straight to the point. "Mr. Butler, I want you to give $40,000 to enlarge the State Hospital in Providence."

He looked hard at this small, ladylike person. She wore a dark dress and her hair was plainly arranged. Yet she was beautiful. Her eyes were shining.

"Miss Dix," Cyrus Butler said. "I had heard of you, and I was ready to turn you down. But you are not the kind of person I expected. I have changed my mind. I'll give you the money you ask if a like amount is given by others."

Dorothea agreed. In a short time she had his check. People called her "the marvel of Rhode Island."

Then she went on to New Jersey. There was no hospital for the insane in the entire state. Dorothea lived in a boardinghouse in Trenton near the state capitol. Every evening for weeks she talked to the state legislators in her parlor. She told them about the sad cases she had seen in New Jersey. She asked them to pass a law for a state hospital.

They listened, but for a long time they did not help her. One evening the leader of the men got up. "You have won me over," he said. "The Lord bless you, Miss Dix!"

Dorothea helped to pick out a place for the New Jersey State Hospital at Trenton. She helped to plan its design. She called this hospital her "first child." It always had a special place in her heart.

Dorothea went on to other states—Pennsylvania, Ohio, and Illinois. She traveled in all kinds of weather.

DOROTHEA DIX

She went by wagon, stagecoach, and riverboat. Sometimes there were long delays. She used the time to read more and more about the latest treatment for mental illness.

In North Carolina she nursed a dying woman in her hotel. She stayed with the woman to the end. Afterward the woman's husband came to her. Tears were running down his face.

"Miss Dix, my wife's last request was to help you get your law passed. I will do everything in my power."

He was one of the most important men in the state legislature!

Soon a hospital for the insane was built in North Carolina. Dorothea was told it would be named Dix Hill in her honor.

"Don't name it for me," she said, "but for my grandfather, Dr. Elijah Dix."

Her fame was growing. She received letters from all over the country asking for her help.

"I must go," she told Ann Heath. Soon she was on her way to Louisiana, Alabama, Georgia, and South Carolina.

Once her stagecoach was held up by a robber. She leaned out the window to ask what was wrong. The masked man heard her.

"That voice!" he said. "I remember! You are Miss Dix.

You spoke to my mother in a hospital in Pennsylvania." Then he shouted to the driver. "Go on! I won't take money from anyone in Miss Dix's company."

Dorothea Dix helped the cause of the mentally ill in every state she visited.

Then a new dream began to form in her mind. The national as well as the state governments should help! Such help would be much greater.

At that time, there were vast empty lands in the West. The government owned them all. Dorothea

Dorothea Dix found her life's work in a crusade for better care of the mentally ill.

wanted the government to sell some of the land. The money could be used to build hospitals for the proper care of the insane.

It was a long, hard struggle to get congressmen and senators to agree. She stayed in Washington, D.C., for four years, talking about and pleading for her land bill. At last, it was passed by a majority vote in both houses of Congress.

The bill was sent to President Pierce. It could not become law without his signature. But the president refused to sign the bill! He said that under this law the federal government would be doing things the states should do. The states should care for their own poor and handicapped, he said.

Dorothea was heartbroken. She felt that her years of work were lost. The law she wanted so much was never passed.

Dorothea went abroad for a long rest. She visited the Rathbones at Greenbank again. Her name was known now all over Europe. She was asked by many countries to visit their hospitals. Soon she was traveling from one to the other. She gave advice to some, but she learned from others. Many hospitals in Europe were ahead of America in caring for their mentally ill people.

Dorothea spent two years abroad. Then she returned to America ready for more work.

9. Civil War Nurse

The next four years were very busy ones for Dorothea. "The more I do for the mentally sick and the poor, the more I see to do," she told Ann Heath.

She helped to start the Hospital for the Insane of the Army and Navy in Washington, D.C. This is now called St. Elizabeth's Hospital.

During these years the North and South were quarreling over slavery. Fiery speeches were made in Congress. Many people felt sure that war was coming.

Dorothea kept on with her work, still hoping that war could be avoided. Though she was against slavery, she traveled through the South raising money for more hospitals there. "My job is to help the insane, both North and South," she said.

In November 1860, Abraham Lincoln was elected president. The Southerners knew Lincoln would not allow slavery to spread. Soon after his election, South Carolina left the Union. Other Southern states joined South Carolina. They claimed that they were a new nation, the Confederate States of America.

There was no fighting, however. Then in April 1861, Southern troops fired on Fort Sumter. President Lincoln called for soldiers to put down the rebellion.

Dorothea was in Trenton visiting the Trenton State Hospital.

"This means civil war," she said when she read the newspaper.

Two regiments of Massachusetts troops started off for Washington. They were attacked by a large mob in Baltimore.

Dorothea heard the news. "I must take the next train south," she said. "There will be wounded to care for."

She went to Washington and offered her services to the War Department. The secretary of war accepted her offer at once. He made her superintendent of United States Army Nurses. Her job was to choose nurses for the Union Army. Soon she would be in charge of the nurses in all the army hospitals.

She fought disease, carelessness, and dirt. Through her efforts, nursing standards in all hospitals were raised. Dorothea did not hesitate to criticize an army doctor if she felt that his hospital was poorly run. Many of the doctors complained to the secretary of war, but the secretary always backed Dorothea.

One day she inspected a hospital near Washington. She pointed out the dirt, the bad food, and the lack of comfort for the sick and wounded soldiers. The doctor was cross. "Madam, who are you to tell me?"

Dorothea drew herself up to her full height. She said proudly, "I am Dorothea L. Dix, superintendent of nurses, in the employ of the United States."

Many women who wanted to be army nurses came to Washington. At that time there were no schools for trained nurses in any of the hospitals. Dorothea Dix was not a trained nurse. She knew more about hospitals, however, than almost any other woman in the country. She also knew what kind of nurses she wanted.

"An army hospital is no place for a girl or woman who does not have good health, courage, and character," she said. "No woman under 30 need apply. All nurses should be plain in dress, with no curls, no jewelry, and no hoopskirts." Her first question to those who came was, "Are you ready to work?"

Dorothea herself worked for four long years without a vacation.

To the suffering men in the hospitals, she was an angel of mercy. She brought them fruit and jellies. She smoothed their pillows and wrote letters for them. Sadly, she sent for relatives when a soldier was dying.

"This war in my own country is breaking my heart," she wrote to Mrs. Rathbone.

In 1862, a tall, brown-haired young woman came to Washington. She asked Miss Dix if she could be an army nurse. She was Louisa May Alcott, who was to become famous later as the author of *Little Women*.

Dorothea liked her plain, sensible look and her willingness to work. She sent Louisa to the Union Hotel, which had been turned into a hospital.

Dorothea was proud of the nurses who worked under her in this Civil War army hospital in Washington.

The young woman worked very hard at her job. Then, after only six weeks, she got pneumonia. Dorothea ordered her to go home.

"Please let me stay," Louisa begged. "I'm sure I will be better soon."

Instead she grew worse. Dorothea sent for Mr. Alcott to come for his daughter. Sadly, Louisa left Washington. Later she wrote about her experiences in a book called *Hospital Sketches*.

At last a day came when shouts and music filled the air. Robert E. Lee, the Confederate general, had surrendered.

That night, the lights in the city of Washington

burned brightly. Dorothea went to her window and watched the happy, singing crowds. She thanked God the war was over.

10. Later Years

Dorothea stayed on in Washington during the long, hot summer. There were still wounded soldiers to nurse. She was also trying to get pensions for nurses who were not well. Some had become sick through their war service.

At last Dorothea returned home to Massachusetts. There she stayed with Ann Heath for a while. Then she visited her brother Joseph and his family.

"Are you ready to retire now, Dolly?" Joseph asked.

Dorothea shook her head. "No indeed. I am going to take up my work again." She smiled. "My real work."

Joseph nodded. He knew that his sister's work for the insane was closest to her heart.

At 65, Dorothea Dix was lively and quick. She looked younger than her age. Soon she was traveling again. She inspected all kinds of places where the mentally ill were kept. She pointed out the need for more hospitals. The war had broken the minds and spirits of many soldiers.

Many of the hospitals for the insane had become run-down during the war years. New hospitals had to be built, and old ones made bigger. Dorothea went from Maine to Florida, from New York to California.

Dorothea worked for fifteen more years. The little old lady in a dark dress, bonnet, and shawl was recognized everywhere. She never had to pay fares on trains or ships. Railroad presidents and owners of steamship lines sent her free passes. She was known and loved by everyone who knew her.

She helped many charities. She was always collecting food, clothing, and other things for needy groups. Children were named for her. Hospitals which she had founded hung her picture on their walls.

Dorothea Dix was nearly 80 years old when she decided to retire. When she became ill, she went to the Trenton State Hospital. There Dorothea Dix spent her last years, in a sunny apartment overlooking the Delaware River.

Dorothea Lynde Dix will always be remembered as a pioneer in providing for the insane. She took up the cause of the most hopeless and neglected people in America. Her courage and devotion to this cause brought about better treatment for the mentally ill, fine hospitals, and above all—hope.

LINDA RICHARDS
1841–1930

In the late eighteen hundreds there was "no place for women in medicine." Linda Richards would not accept this. It took courage to fight the entire medical profession, but Linda had courage to spare. She met ignorance and prejudice head-on to become America's first trained nurse. Her life's work of setting up training schools for other women raised nursing to professional status. And her new ideas for nursing patients back to health changed hospitals forever. As medical knowledge increased, Linda insisted nursing care keep pace. Teaching, inspecting, modifying, improving, Linda Richards continued her courageous battle around the world.

Linda Richards
First American Trained Nurse

by David R. Collins

Copyright © 1973
by David R. Collins

1. "Teach Me More"

Christmas Day, 1850.

A light snow blew across the fields of Vermont. Set between low hills, a frozen lake sparkled in the sun. The cold air rang with the shouts and laughter of boys and girls skating in circles on the ice.

In a small gray farmhouse nearby, nine-year-old Linda Richards watched the fun from a bedroom window. She smiled and waved at three of her friends walking by toward the lake.

"Linda," called a weak voice from across the room. "Linda, I dropped my pills."

Linda turned and hurried toward the bed in the corner.

"Oh, mama, you shouldn't try to get them," she said. "I'll take care of you."

As a young girl Linda Richards many times said the words "I'll take care of you." But she did not know that with those words she was setting the pattern for her life.

Melinda Ann Judson Richards was born July 27, 1841, on a farm near Potsdam, New York. When Linda was four years old, her father moved the family west to Wisconsin. He built a log cabin and cleared land for a farm.

Linda liked her new home. With her two older sisters, Laura and Elizabeth, Linda shared many adventures. Some days the three girls picked berries and climbed trees. Other times they went wading in streams. Each of the girls had her own hiding places in the nearby woods.

But the happy days in Wisconsin did not last. One night Mr. Richards suddenly became ill. By morning he was dead. Sadly Mrs. Richards brought her three girls back East. She bought a small farm outside Newport, Vermont, near the farm of Linda's Grandpa Sinclair.

Within a few weeks Mrs. Richards also became ill. Grandpa Sinclair drove his buggy over and helped with the outside work. The three girls shared the chores inside the farmhouse before and after school.

Laura, who was fourteen, divided the duties among her sisters and herself. The list was long. There was little playtime for thirteen-year-old Elizabeth and nine-year-old Linda. The three girls had to make and mend clothes, cook meals, scrub floors, wash dishes, pump water, and churn butter. They all tried to care for Mrs. Richards, but Linda seemed to be the best nurse.

"Eat just a bite more," Linda would coax her mother at mealtime. "And drink a bit of hot broth."

Without being told, Linda knew the best way to fix the pillows. She seemed to know when her mother wanted a shawl around her shoulders.

Old Doc Currier, who had an office in Newport, stopped by weekly at the Richards house. On one visit he watched Linda as she arranged the medicines on a bedside table.

"You do more good for your mother than my medicine," Doc Currier said. "But don't forget to look after yourself, child. Try to keep up with your school lessons. That will help keep your mother happy too."

Linda followed Doc Currier's orders. Every night after supper she read her lessons with Laura and Elizabeth.

Even with Linda's care, Mrs. Richards grew weaker. One spring night she called her three daughters into her room. Quietly the sick woman talked about the happy days in Wisconsin. Then, with her children beside her, Mrs. Richards died.

For many days Linda was too unhappy to talk. She did not want to eat. Sleep came after hours of crying. It was old Doc Currier who finally comforted the sad young girl.

One day he found Linda sitting alone on the front steps. He sat down beside her.

"Linda, you did all you could," he said kindly. "You did more than any one of us to help your mother."

Linda shook her head.

"But it still wasn't enough," she said.

"You did everything you knew to do."

Linda looked up at the old doctor.

"I want to know more. I want to help other people who are sick. Will you teach me more?"

"I'd like to do that, Linda. Let's talk about it again when you're a little older."

2. Barnyard Hospital

New homes were found for the Richards girls. Laura went to Boston to live with cousins. Elizabeth and Linda moved in with Grandpa and Grandma Sinclair.

Elizabeth helped Grandma Sinclair with the housework. Linda enjoyed helping grandpa with the farm animals. Soon all the animals seemed like friends to her.

As she milked the cows or fed the horses, she talked to them and called them by name. When she gathered the eggs, the hens seemed to cluck a greeting. Whatever chore she was doing, she had good company. Her pet rooster followed her everywhere on the farm.

When Linda wasn't helping with the farm chores, Grandpa Sinclair knew where to find her. One corner of the barn was special to Linda. There she cared for her animal "patients."

"If I get sick, will you take good care of me like that?" Grandpa Sinclair teased as he watched Linda spoon-feed a baby rabbit.

Doc Currier stopped by as often as he could. He enjoyed watching Linda work with the animals.

"You've got a good barnyard hospital here," he laughed. "I wouldn't mind being a sick cow on this farm."

"You're just like grandpa," Linda said. "I'm glad my animal patients don't tease me all the time."

Other people heard about Linda's barnyard hospital. Soon she was caring for pet dogs, pet cats, and even a pet goat.

Then, on her thirteenth birthday, Linda received a surprise present. Doc Currier stopped by and asked her to go with him on some sick calls.

Doc had remembered her wish! Linda scrambled up into the buggy, eager to get started.

In the months that followed Doc Currier often came to pick up his new helper. Sometimes they left the Sinclair house at sunrise and did not return until dark. As the buggy bumped along over the dirt roads, Linda asked questions.

"What is the best way to stop bleeding?"

"How can you tell if a bone is really broken?"

Doc Currier answered each question carefully. He knew Linda would try to remember every word he said.

At first Linda did only little tasks like boiling water and ripping bandage cloths. But before a year had passed, Doc Currier had shown her how to set splints on broken bones, clean wounds, and apply bandages.

"Treating sick people calls for calm and careful thinking," Doc Currier told Linda often. "Decide what needs to be done for your patient and do it. Sometimes you'll feel frightened. Just don't let your fear

Country doctors traveled great distances to make house calls in the mid-1800s. Linda became Doc Currier's willing helper on his rounds.

show. Your patient must trust you and have faith in you. Don't forget that."

One cold night a strange buggy stopped in front of the Sinclair farmhouse. Without tying his horse to the post, the driver leaped up the porch steps. He pounded on the door.

"We can't find Doc Currier," the worried young man told Grandpa Sinclair. "My wife said to come here and bring back the Richards girl who helps Doc. My boy's sick—real sick."

Linda heard the man. Even before grandpa could call her, she was putting on her coat. Soon Linda was hurrying through the doorway of a tiny white farmhouse. In the bedroom a woman sat beside a young boy.

"Oh, thank heavens, you've come. Tommy's so hot. He won't open his eyes. I don't know what to do."

Linda barely heard the woman's words. She saw that Tommy's skin was dry. The boy was restless under the heavy quilt.

Linda tried to remember everything Doc Currier had told her about fever. She had never taken care of a patient without him. She was frightened, but there was no time to lose. She slipped off her coat and tossed it onto a nearby chair.

"We've got to break this fever," Linda declared, rolling up her sleeves. "We'll need chipped ice and towels."

Tommy's father hurried out into the snowy yard to hunt for chunks of ice. The boy's mother and Linda got the towels ready.

Moments later Linda filled a towel with ice chips. Then she stroked Tommy's head and chest with the cool, damp cloth.

Hour after hour Linda went on with the ice baths. By morning her own body was tired and aching. But Tommy seemed cooler and more comfortable.

At last Doc Currier came. Linda ran to the door to meet him.

"I tried not to be afraid," she whispered in Doc's ear. "But I was—at first."

Slowly Doc Currier examined Tommy and asked Linda a few questions. Finally the old man stood up.

"Tommy is going to be just fine," he said. "He's a strong boy, and he's had a good nurse here. She did everything for him I could have done."

Linda felt happy at Doc's words. She knew she would never again be afraid to treat a patient.

3. The New Schoolmistress

The passing years brought many changes to the Sinclair farm. Grandma Sinclair died. Elizabeth married and moved away. Only Grandpa Sinclair and Linda were left.

"Linda, I've been thinking about your future," grandpa said one morning. "What's to become of you after I'm gone? I can't count on too many more years at my age."

Linda stopped clearing the breakfast dishes. She opened her mouth to speak. Grandpa did not give her the chance.

"I think this fall you should go to St. Johnsbury Academy. When you finish, you'll be able to teach."

"But I don't want to teach," Linda said. "I want to stay here with you."

Grandpa shook his head. "It would help me to know you're able to look after yourself. Anyway, I would feel proud if you were a teacher."

Linda accepted Grandpa Sinclair's wishes. At fifteen she enrolled in St. Johnsbury Academy. The school was thirty miles from Newport.

The year Linda spent at St. Johnsbury was an unhappy one. She hated the many lectures and daily tests. News of Doc Currier's death brought more sadness into the dreary year. Linda barely passed the state exams given at the end of the spring term. She was glad to return to the farm.

Linda wanted to teach near Newport so she could live with grandpa. Luckily she was hired as schoolmistress of the school she had once attended.

Linda braided her long dark hair and piled it high

on her head. She wanted to look taller. She fixed up some of Grandma Sinclair's old dresses to wear.

A happy surprise greeted Linda on her first day at the schoolhouse. Many of her pupils were her old friends.

"Remember when you and Doc Currier fixed my leg?" one boy asked. "I'm going to pay you back by being good in school. Mama said I should."

"You and Doc Currier cured my sore throat," a girl with freckles said. "You took care of my baby doll too. Do you remember?"

Yes, Linda remembered. Linda often thought back to the house calls she had made with Doc Currier. How happy and useful those days had been!

Linda had been teaching for only a year when Grandpa Sinclair died. In 1858 Linda sold the farm. Like other teachers of the time, she went to live with first one family, then another. Families were glad to give Linda a free room and meals in exchange for her teaching services.

In the summer of 1860 Linda went to live with an old widow outside Newport. Widow Poole was well known for her good cooking. No one enjoyed her fine meals more than her nephew George.

George Poole came to visit his aunt often. Linda liked him from the first time they met. George always had a funny story to tell. He took Linda ice skating and sledding. They sang songs in front of the fireplace. Linda liked being with George. When he asked her to marry him, Linda accepted. A May wedding date was set.

But one afternoon in April George came to the house early. He had bad news. Southern soldiers had fired on a United States Army fort filled with Northern soldiers. War was coming.

"Will you have to fight?" Linda asked.

"If President Lincoln calls for volunteers," George answered, "it would be my duty to go."

The call for volunteers came three days later. George Poole was among the first to sign up.

The Civil War lasted four years, and a million lives were lost. George Poole was badly wounded in the fighting. When he came home, he was weak and sickly. Once again Linda had a patient to nurse.

For almost five years Linda helped care for George. But George refused to marry her.

"I will not make you a bride one day and a widow the next," he said. His death in the winter of 1869 was a blow to Linda.

"My life is empty and without real meaning," she wrote to a friend. "Teaching is not the answer for me. It offers me no real happiness. I only hope I can find some useful purpose for my life."

Linda Richards decided that caring for the sick

was the most useful work she could do. But if she were going to be a nurse, she wanted to be a good one. She knew she must find a place to get the training she needed.

4. On to Boston

Linda gripped her suitcase tightly as she stepped from the train in Boston. She knew no one in this big city. She had no place to work. She had no place to live. Linda was twenty-nine years old. She had been on her own for more than ten years. Still, she felt frightened. How long would her small savings last here?

Suddenly Linda remembered old Doc Currier's words: "Just don't let your fear show." Quickly Linda hurried out among the groups of strangers and into the street.

Linda had never seen so many tall buildings. She knew that some of them were hospitals and schools. Surely in one of them she could find the training she wanted. This hope made her forget her fear.

Linda found a room in a small boardinghouse. The owner was a friendly woman named Mrs. Higgens. She invited Linda to have a cup of tea with her, and soon Linda was talking about her plans. Mrs. Higgens looked doubtful.

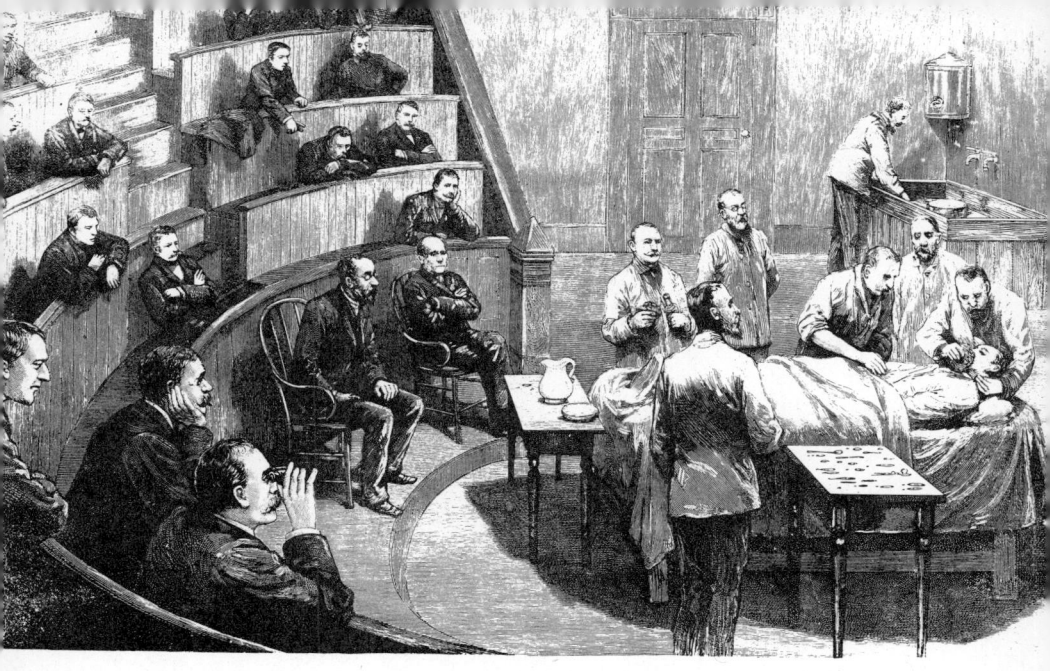

The care of hospital patients was "men's work" when Linda arrived in Boston. Operations were usually performed by male doctors aided by male orderlies.

"In England there are programs for training nurses," the landlady said. She sipped her warm tea. "I know of none in our country. Many doctors have boarded in my house, and I have heard their talk. I am quite certain that not one of them would have taken time to train women nurses."

"But what of the women who nursed the soldiers on the Civil War battlefields? Women nurses were useful then. Why couldn't they be useful now?"

Mrs. Higgens shook her head.

"The war is over now. Men believe that women belong in their homes, not in hospitals."

Linda refused to accept such an idea. She began looking for a nursing position in Boston's hospitals. Some doctors would not speak with her. Those who did were often rude.

"Me? Train a woman as a nurse? Never!" one doctor said.

"You have trained as a teacher," was another doctor's reply. "Go home and teach!"

Linda kept looking. She pleaded for any job that would give her hospital training. Finally she was offered work as a ward maid in the Boston City Hospital. The pay was only seven dollars a month, and she could not take care of sick people.

Still, she would be near the doctors and patients. She could learn by watching and listening. Linda took the job.

Linda began her duties at five o'clock every morning. She swept and scrubbed the floors. Then she washed windows, dusted, ironed sheets, and helped cook meals. Whenever she could she did favors for the patients.

One morning Linda brought a young boy a drink of water. Another ward maid was watching. She walked over to Linda and nudged her sharply in the side.

"Do the work you are told to do. Don't try to get out of your work by fussin' with the patients."

"What kind of hospital is this where the floors are treated better than the patients?" Linda wondered. She was more determined than ever to get some training.

The next morning Linda went to the head matron. She asked the older woman to teach her all that she had learned about caring for sick people. The head matron wanted to help. But she knew little more than Linda did.

Again and again Linda begged the doctors for help. Many of them laughed at her. A few became angry.

"You women are to take care of the cleaning. We will take care of the patients," one doctor declared.

"We could clean the hospital and help you too if you would teach us," Linda answered firmly.

Linda worked sixteen hours a day, six days a week. She had no time to learn by watching the doctors. The head matron could not help her. Worn out and discouraged, she gave up her job.

"Get some rest and come back to us," the hospital director said. "We need good workers."

"A good worker. That's all I have been," Linda thought. "But I want to be more than that. I want to be a good nurse!"

As she rested and grew stronger, Linda read every book she could find about nursing. Stories about Florence Nightingale and her nursing programs in

England gave Linda new hope. If only such programs could be brought to America!

At last Linda felt strong enough to begin her search for training again. A sign posted in a Boston bookstore caught her attention one day.

TRAINING PROGRAM FOR NURSES
OPENING SOON
THE NEW ENGLAND HOSPITAL FOR
WOMEN AND CHILDREN
PLEASANT STREET
BOSTON, MASSACHUSETTS

Linda hurried to Pleasant Street and found the hospital. She walked to the door and knocked.

"I've come about your training program for nurses," Linda said to the woman who opened the door.

"Just a moment," the woman answered. "I'll call Dr. Dimock. You may come into the parlor."

As she waited Linda wondered about this doctor. Why had he decided women should be trained as nurses? Maybe he had come from England.

Linda heard the parlor door open. In walked a tall young woman wearing a brown dress.

"I am Dr. Susan Dimock," she said. "I understand you have come about our training program for nurses."

A woman doctor? Linda was speechless.

"I—I'm sorry. I just didn't expect to meet a woman doctor."

Dr. Dimock smiled. "There are only a few of us in this country. If you're planning to become a nursing student, I hope you won't mind working with women doctors."

"If you don't mind working with women nurses," Linda laughed, "I won't mind working with women doctors."

5. Nursing School at Last

The nurses' training school was not going to open until fall. Linda did not want to wait so long to get started. She asked Dr. Dimock for summer work at the hospital.

"We could use more help," Dr. Dimock agreed. "The hospital will be moving to a new building in October. But we have so little money. All we could give you would be meals and a bed—"

"I accept," Linda said quickly.

Linda became the hospital errand girl. She wrote letters for the patients and read to them too. She helped cook meals and clean the hospital rooms.

On the morning of September 1, 1872, Linda was pounding nails into a wooden box. Moving day was only a few weeks away.

"Could you come into my office a minute, Linda?" Dr. Dimock called from her doorway.

Linda set the hammer and nails down. Wiping her damp face with her apron, she hurried into Dr. Dimock's office.

"I have something I want you to sign," Dr. Dimock said. She handed Linda a short piece of paper. "This is the day we begin our program for training nurses. Or had you forgotten?"

Linda shook her head as she took the enrollment form. She had looked forward to this moment for a long time. She signed the paper with the happy feeling that at last she was on her way.

"Linda, we are pleased that you are our first student nurse," Dr. Dimock said. "I know you will make us proud."

Soon four more women enrolled, and Dr. Dimock met with the five new students to explain the program. The young women were to wear simple housedresses and slippers. They must get up at 5:30 A.M. and stay on duty until 9:00 P.M. Each student nurse was to take care of six patients day and night. Each would receive one dollar a week for her services.

Early in the program the student nurses were taught to count pulse and breathing rates. Soon they learned to read and record temperatures. They were shown how to measure and give medication.

Doctors gave speeches during the year. Each student nurse was expected to listen, watch, and remember everything she saw and heard.

The daily work was tiring, and the nights brought more problems. Again and again patients would call for their tired, sleepy nurses. Often the young women had only two or three hours of rest. Finally Linda went to Dr. Dimock.

"If one nurse could care for two wards during the night, the other could have a full night's rest. We could take turns sleeping and staying up," Linda said.

Dr. Dimock tried the plan at once and found that it worked well.

One night Linda was sent to the home of a patient ill with pneumonia. A male doctor was treating the sick man when Linda arrived.

"I don't approve of women nurses," the doctor snapped. "You can be of little use to this patient."

Linda took off her cape and stood beside the patient's bed.

"If I can be of little use, it is better than no use at all," Linda said. "I will do my best to follow your orders."

The doctor liked Linda's answer. He agreed to let her try. For the next week Linda visited the patient twice a day. She cooked meals and gave medicine. She changed bedding and gave baths.

A physician teaches students how to apply bandages in an early training school for nurses.

When the doctor made his next call he was pleased.

"This man is almost all well. I truly didn't think you could do it," he told Linda.

"I am glad you think I have helped your patient," Linda said with dignity.

"*Our* patient," the doctor declared. "Yours *and* mine."

Before she knew it, Linda found herself at the end of the year's training. Again she was called to Dr. Dimock's office.

"Linda, this diploma shows you have successfully completed our nurses' training course. I am happy to give it to you." Dr. Dimock smiled. "You have done a fine job here. You have worked hard and have always given more than we asked of you. Your patients trust you and know that you care about them. I hope all our future students will try to do as well."

Linda stared at the words on the diploma. Graduation day—September 1, 1873. At the age of thirty-two Linda was about to start a new life.

As news of Linda's graduation reached hospitals, offers of jobs began arriving. Not many doctors were willing to train nurses, but some were beginning to see that nurses could be useful. Linda read each offer carefully. After days of thought she made up her mind. She accepted the job of night nursing superintendent at the Bellevue Hospital Training School in

New York City. Once again Linda knew she would be a stranger in a big city, but she was not afraid. The diploma—that piece of paper that said she was a "trained nurse"—made her feel she would succeed.

6. Battles to Win

Linda shuddered as she looked up at the huge building before her. The big iron gates seemed to shut the dark place off from the rest of the world.

Inside the hospital walls the patients also seemed shut off. They were the poor and hopeless people of New York City.

"I wish we could break down the walls of this place," Linda told the nursing director. "It's like an old tomb."

Sister Helen Bowden listened quietly. A member of the English All Saints Order, she had studied nursing in London. She was trying to build a new program at Bellevue.

"Yes, it would be good to have a new hospital," she told Linda. "But there are other battles to win first." Sister Helen's voice rose in anger. "Our patients must be treated like human beings. You will learn soon enough what I mean."

Linda's first lesson came when she went on duty that night. The hospital gaslights were turned so low she couldn't make out the faces of the patients. All heat in the hospital was turned off at midnight. Linda looked for more blankets. There were none. For hours the patients shivered in the cold and darkness. Linda did her best to comfort them. Suddenly the heat was turned on. The pipes cracked and rattled, waking everyone.

The next day Linda burst into Sister Helen's office.

"How can patients get well in a hospital where they freeze every night!" Linda cried. "Why must the lights be turned so low? How can student nurses be trained in a place like this?"

Sister Helen shook her head. "The members of the hospital board give the orders. They order the lights lowered. They order the heat turned off. They tell us to save money."

"Then we must show them the value of saving lives," said Linda.

Linda and Sister Helen became fighting partners. They went to every board meeting to ask for changes in the hospital.

Slowly the board members gave in. Lights and heat were left on. A care center was opened so mothers and their new babies would not be near sick patients.

"I am both a pupil and teacher here," Linda wrote to Dr. Dimock. "I am learning many of the Nightingale training methods from Sister Helen. I teach classes every morning. Our student nurses are a cheerful group. One of them has made a uniform which the others are now copying. It is a white and blue striped dress. A happy sight it is! It has a white collar, cuffs, and apron. A small white cap is worn so patients can see the students from a distance."

Student nurses at other training schools in America heard of the Bellevue uniforms. Before long each school of student nurses had its own uniform.

Linda thought it would be a good idea to keep a chart beside each patient's bed. Each time a nurse

A Bellevue Hospital ward in the 1870s. Members of the nursing staff are assisting doctors in surgery.

checked on a patient she marked the chart. When the doctor came, he could see at a glance whether the patient was getting better or worse. Soon other hospitals learned of the bed-chart idea and began using it.

At the end of Linda's year at Bellevue, Sister Helen urged her to stay on. But Linda felt she must help other hospitals set up nursing programs.

"There are battles to be won in many places," she told her partner. "I know you will keep fighting them here."

Linda was asked to lead the training program at the Massachusetts General Hospital. The program there was only one year old, and it was not going well. Linda sensed a challenge, so she accepted the job.

When she arrived at Massachusetts General, she found the doctors wanted nothing to do with a training school for nurses.

"It's a waste of time," they said.

Linda bristled when she heard such comments. Yet she kept her temper, for she wanted to win the doctors' friendship. Besides, Linda had a plan.

She invited relatives and friends of the doctors to afternoon teas. Members of the hospital board were guests too.

"You are all interested in Massachusetts General Hospital," Linda told those attending. "So am I. So are the student nurses who are with us today. I'm sure you'll want to hear about the work they hope to do in the hospital."

The student nurses were excited about their work. They talked for hours with their guests.

"If the doctors help teach us, the patients will receive better care. We will ease the doctors' work load too," said the student nurses.

Linda's plan worked. Her guests went back to the doctors to urge them to help the eager young students. Finally, the doctors agreed.

With the help of the doctors, Linda set up a one-year program for training nurses. New workers were hired to clean and cook—jobs the student nurses once had to do.

"Now let us prove how useful we can be," Linda told her classes.

When her first class of student nurses graduated in 1875, Linda watched with a happy smile. Her smile was even brighter as she looked around at the doctors. They were all proud of *their* school for nurses.

More training schools were opening in America each year. Many of them wanted Linda to help plan their programs. But Linda was ready for a change.

For a long time Linda had heard about the Nightingale Training School in London. Now and then visitors from America were allowed to go there to learn about the programs. Linda wrote a letter asking if she might be accepted.

Months went by. No answer came. Linda had almost given up hope. Then a letter arrived from London.

> My dear Miss Richards,
> The Nightingale Training School at St. Thomas's Hospital would be happy to have you as a visitor. We shall look forward to meeting you.

7. A Special Invitation

Linda sailed from New York City in April 1877. A tall stranger was waiting to meet her at the dock in England.

"I am Mr. Rathbone from the school at St. Thomas's," the man said. He took Linda to his carriage. "We are happy to welcome you to England. My cousin, Miss Florence Nightingale, sends her special greetings."

Linda's face showed surprise. She hadn't expected such attention from the famous Miss Nightingale.

A few days later Linda received another surprise—a note inviting her to lunch. The invitation was signed by Florence Nightingale.

Linda slept little the night before the luncheon. She

was too excited. Again and again she changed her mind about what dress to wear. She scolded herself as she braided her hair into a soft bun at the back of her head.

"You are 36 years old, not a schoolgirl of 10," Linda told herself. "You are just going to pay a visit to another nurse."

Still, as she walked up the front steps of Florence Nightingale's house on South Street, Linda's heart beat faster. A maid led her into the sitting room.

Florence Nightingale was resting on a small velvet couch. She was almost sixty, but her face was smooth and without the usual lines of age.

"Miss Richards, I am so happy you could come," she said with a smile.

Linda suddenly was at ease. At once she felt Florence Nightingale was her friend.

All afternoon the two women talked. Miss Nightingale helped Linda make plans for learning about the Nightingale program.

The study began at St. Thomas's Training School. Linda was met by the matron, Mrs. Wardroper.

"We want you to stay right here with us at the nurses' home," said Mrs. Wardroper. "You will spend one week in each of our hospital's eight wards. You may work or watch as you choose. You may attend all surgical operations and staff meetings."

Florence Nightingale

Linda reported for duty early the next morning in the children's ward.

"You must be the American nurse," one doctor declared. "Jolly good! Glad to have you with us."

Linda nodded. She was happy the doctors seemed so kind. There was so much she wanted to learn.

At St. Thomas's Linda worked in each of the eight wards. Every day she spent a busy twelve hours on duty. Then, at night in her room, Linda kept her desk lamp burning late as she wrote down all she had seen and heard.

"Both the patient and doctor trust the nurses here," she wrote. "I believe this trust helps the nurses carry out their duties."

Linda visited other hospitals. Sometimes she went to nursing classes. Other times she worked in the hospital wards. Always she carried a notebook in her apron pocket.

"You must get tired of writing," one nurse said.

Linda nodded. "It's just that I don't want to forget anything. We in America have much to learn from you."

As Linda's stay in England ended, she received another invitation from Florence Nightingale to spend a few days at her summer home.

Linda was happy to see Miss Nightingale again. Each afternoon they met for tea and talked in the garden. The two women became good friends.

From England, Linda went to Paris. There she spent a month visiting hospitals and schools. But now she was eager to return to America to share what she had learned. In October 1877 Linda sailed for home.

8. Journey to Japan

Good news was waiting for Linda on her arrival in America. Six more hospitals had started training programs for nurses. Another was ready to begin at Boston City Hospital. The hospital director asked Linda to lead the program.

"Most of our doctors are against the idea of a training school for nurses," said Dr. Cowles. "You'll have a lot of hard work here. Getting the doctors to help will be the hardest part. But I will do all I can."

It was not an easy decision for Linda. She remembered how unhappy she had been at Boston City Hospital. But she could not say no to a challenge.

"I accept your offer," Linda told Dr. Cowles. "We'll show those other doctors how useful good nurses can be!"

Linda set up a two-year program for training nurses. She used many ideas she had learned in England.

Since the Boston City Hospital doctors would not help, Linda looked for teachers in other places. She brought in graduate nurses from other hospitals to lead classes. Linda taught some of the classes too.

Often after class a group of students gathered around Linda to talk. She listened to their problems. She gave them good advice.

"Always remember, the care of your patient must come first," she told her students. "You must hide your own problems when you are working. Be ready to help the doctors quickly whenever they need you."

The young women soon learned to love and respect Linda. They listened eagerly to all she told them.

Slowly the students began to win the trust of the doctors. More and more duties were given the new nurses. Finally the doctors agreed to help.

Once the program was accepted and running well, Linda began to look around for a new task. She heard that someone was needed to set up a nursing program in Japan. Linda volunteered for the job.

"I know nothing of the Japanese language or customs," she said. "But I'm willing to help if I can."

Linda was accepted. She sailed for Japan in December 1885.

Before she started to plan the nursing program, Linda studied the Japanese language. Before long she could speak well enough to begin teaching.

But not all Japanese customs came so easily. After watching her fumble with her chopsticks while eating, Linda's friends gave her a special gift.

"Linda, here is a wooden spoon," they said. "The food you can keep on your chopsticks wouldn't keep an ant alive."

"You've probably saved me from death by starvation," she admitted with a hearty laugh.

The school for nurses was set up in a small mission hospital in Kyoto. It was Linda's job to plan a two-year program. She was pleased to find she would have the help of two American mission doctors and six Japanese doctors.

Five students enrolled in the first class. They shared two tiny rooms behind the kitchen in the mission hospital. Linda had her own little room upstairs near three small rooms for the hospital patients.

"Our school and hospital is tiny," Linda told the new students. "But sometimes a tiny bottle of medicine can do much good."

Linda spoke slowly in Japanese. Often it was easier for her to explain things in English. She was happy to find that two of the students spoke English and could help the other three.

While the students learned more about nursing, Linda learned more about Japanese customs. She discovered that the student nurses were sometimes afraid of the men patients.

"In Japan a woman never tells a Japanese man what to do," a student told Linda one day. "Today my patient won't take his medicine."

Linda had long ago learned to handle all kinds of problems with patients.

"Come with me," she said, leading the way to a mat where a Japanese man lay. "Now, when the nurse gives you medicine, it is what the doctor has told her to do," she said to the man. "The nurse is not telling you to take medicine. The doctor is."

Linda learned to go from place to place by rickshaw as her Japanese friends did.

The man nodded and took the medicine willingly. His dignity was saved.

"Ah, that is better," the student smiled.

The mission hospital and school for nurses in Kyoto grew fast. Linda went into the city and taught home nursing to other Japanese students.

Linda stayed in Japan for five years. Then an ear ailment began to bother her. The hospital doctors said she should return to America.

With some sadness Linda packed her bags. She smiled as she slipped the old wooden spoon into her suitcase. She would miss her Japanese friends.

9. Home Nursing

A brisk November wind snapped at Linda's dark cape as she hurried along the Philadelphia street. Linda looked again at the numbers on the nearby tenement houses.

"Down here, lady!" a child called out from the front steps of one of the houses.

Quickly Linda walked down the steps to a basement doorway. She smiled at the little girl who had come to the visiting nurse's office that morning.

"Where is your papa?" Linda asked.

"Come. I take you to him." The girl took Linda's hand and led her inside. "Papa will not be happy that I bring you. He thinks you ladies snoop in our houses. He thinks you laugh at us for being poor."

Linda shook her head. "We want only to help you if we can. I will talk with your papa. Don't be frightened."

On a cot in the next room Linda found the man tossing in a restless sleep. Linda stepped closer. She could see a deep and dirty cut between two of the fingers on his right hand. Red streaks shot up his badly swollen arm.

Suddenly the man's eyes opened.

"Who are you? What do you want here?" he asked.

"I am Miss Richards of the Philadelphia Visiting

Nurses." Linda set her nursing bag on a table. "I have come to help you. Please let me see—"

"Get out! Get out of here!" the man shouted. "If I wanted help, I would send for a doctor."

It was hopeless to argue. Linda took her bag and left. But in an hour she was back—with a doctor. He examined the man's wound and turned to Linda.

"The wound is just as you told me, Miss Richards. The treatment you plan to use is exactly right. Yes, by all means put hot, wet cloths on the wound to draw the poison. When the poison has gathered, open the wound."

"This—this woman can do that?" the patient asked.

"Probably better than I could!" the doctor laughed. "Now you do as she says."

Linda had joined the Philadelphia Visiting Nurses Society soon after returning from Japan. The nurses traveled all over the city to care for sick people in their homes. Most of their work was done in poor areas of the city. Linda liked that, for she felt most useful when she was helping the poor.

The Philadelphia society had its share of problems. The visiting nurses needed money for their work. The money was given by wealthy families in the city. Some people began saying the visiting nurses could not be "of good character." They said no nice woman would go about the city alone and into the homes

Visiting nurses starting on their rounds at the turn of the century. Linda joined these dedicated women in bringing medical care to the slums.

of poor strangers. Also, many of the poor families did not trust the nurses who offered free help.

Linda became head nurse in April 1891. She attacked the problems right away.

Linda called at the homes of the wealthy families. She told the people of the work of the visiting nurses.

Often Linda met with the visiting nurses. "When you enter a home, do nothing but care for your patient. Do not speak about or even notice other things in the home," she told them.

Slowly the stories about the visiting nurses disappeared. The poor families began to welcome them.

But for Linda the price of success had been high. The home visits, the long reports that had to be written, the direction of the program—all had tired her.

Once again Linda had worked so hard that she became ill. Now 50, she had nursed for many long and wearing years. She knew that she must rest for a while. But she also knew that before long there would be a new challenge. And when it came she would not be able to say no.

10. A Final Task

Linda listened quietly to the two men who had come to see her. They wanted her to become director of nurses at a hospital for the mentally ill.

"I would like to help you," Linda said. "But I don't know if I have the skills for the work you want done."

"Let *us* judge your skills, Miss Richards. We know you can help us."

Linda could not refuse. As the nineteenth century ended, Linda became director of nurses at a mental hospital in Taunton, Massachusetts.

Linda worked closely with the doctors. They tried new ways of treating the mentally ill patients. Linda shared what she learned with the student nurses.

"Take time to listen to your patients," Linda told the students. "Help them to become interested in doing something. Be gentle and kind. These people are lonely and afraid, but do not pity them. Talk with them. They must feel you care about them."

Linda spent little time in her office. She liked working with the patients.

One day as a doctor walked out of the hospital he saw Linda high on a ladder against a tree. Three patients were firmly holding the ladder.

"Miss Richards, what are you doing?" the doctor called.

"I am hanging our birdhouses," Linda called down. "We made them in the hospital workshop."

The nurses at Taunton followed Linda's example. They spent time talking with the patients and helping them do small chores.

Linda helped start nursing programs for the mentally ill at other hospitals. But the years were slipping by. Linda knew she could not keep up the busy pace of her younger days. In 1911, at 70, Linda gave up active nursing.

Linda went to live quietly with friends in Foxboro, Massachusetts. She was always glad to welcome guests but seldom left her house.

In 1928 Linda became ill and was taken to a nursing home. When the nurses at the New England Hospital for Women and Children heard of Linda's illness, they begged her to come stay with them.

So it was that Linda returned to the hospital from which she had graduated as America's first trained nurse. She died there April 16, 1930.

Newspapers across the country carried the news of Linda's death. Some noted the final words of her autobiography, which was published in 1912:

> As for my own work, I often feel that, for the many years I have served, I have accomplished little. Whether I have been a wise builder, someone else must decide.

Was Linda a "wise builder"?

For the answer, one has only to look at the profession of nursing today.

HELEN KELLER
1880–1968

Helen Keller had two strikes against her. She was deaf and blind. But into her dark and soundless world there came a miracle. The miracle was teacher Anne Sullivan. With Anne Sullivan's help, Helen fought courageously to free herself from a lonely life. Not only did she overcome the tremendous difficulties of learning to live without sight or hearing, but she dedicated herself to helping others. There were many dark hours. But for her it was worth the effort to be part of life. Through her courageous example and unselfish crusade to create better understanding for the handicapped, Helen Keller did more for the silent and sightless of the world than anyone who has ever lived.

Helen Keller
Toward the Light

by Stewart and Polly Anne Graff

Copyright © 1965
by Stewart Graff
and Polly Anne Graff

1. Darkness

One afternoon a little girl sat on the porch steps of her home. It was her sixth birthday, June 27, in the year 1886. The house was in the small town of Tuscumbia, Alabama.

The little girl had curly golden hair. Her bare arms and legs were sturdy. But there was something strange about her eyes. When she stared into the bright sun, she did not blink.

Roses bloomed in the arbor. Across the yard, a pony whinnied in the pasture. It would have been a nice afternoon to ride, but the little girl sat alone. There was a strange, angry expression on her face.

She could feel the warm sun, but she could not see anything but blackness because she was blind. She could smell the roses, but she could not see their color. She could not hear her pony whinny, because she was deaf also.

The little girl's name was Helen Keller. She lived with her parents and her baby sister Mildred in a comfortable house with wide fields and a big barn.

Helen's father had been a captain in the Civil War. Now he owned a newspaper.

When Helen Keller was born, she could see and hear like other children. But when she was a year and a half old, she became very ill. Fever burned her small body. The doctors could not help. Her mother and father were afraid Helen would die.

At last Helen got better, but the fever left a terrible mark. When her mother brought a lamp, Helen did not look at the bright light. When her father clapped his hands loudly, she did not turn toward the sound. Then they knew that their little girl was blind and deaf.

Helen was soon well and strong again. When she grew older, she wanted to run and play. But when she ran, she crashed into trees and fences or fell and hurt herself.

Other children were afraid to play with her because she often hit them roughly and broke their toys. Even Belle, the family's setter dog, ran away from her. Helen did not understand that other people had feelings too. Once she pushed her baby sister out of her cradle.

Worst of all, Helen could not speak or understand others. Her mind was bright and active. She could feel her way quickly through the house or follow the path to the barn. She learned a few signs. She would pull or push to mean "come" or "go." She could show her mother that she was hungry or thirsty.

But Helen could not hear voices. She could not see people talking. She did not know that people talked in *words*.

Sitting on the porch steps, Helen was restless and lonely. She did not know it was her birthday. She did not know that her mother was baking her a cake.

Suddenly the screen door slammed. Helen turned. She could not hear the slam, but it made a shake. It was a vibration that she could feel. She felt the tap-tap of her mother's footsteps.

Mrs. Keller had come to dress Helen for supper. But when Helen sniffed the smell of freshly baked cake, she ran past her mother. She felt her way quickly to the kitchen and grabbed at the cake. She stuffed warm chunks in her mouth.

Mrs. Keller hurried after Helen. She took the cake away and put it out of reach. Helen was angry. She loved sweets, and she was used to eating anything she wanted. She did not know the cake was for her birthday supper. She kicked and screamed. She fell on the floor sobbing.

Before her mother could stop her, Helen rushed outdoors. She ran wildly into a bramble bush. The thorns scraped her face. She tripped and fell. A sharp stone cut her knee.

Mrs. Keller carried Helen back inside. She bandaged Helen's knee and put her to bed. The birthday cake was spoiled. Helen was worn out with temper and crying. She was alone in the darkness again.

Downstairs Helen's mother and father ate their supper sadly. Mrs. Keller told her husband what had just happened. "Helen's tempers are growing worse," Mrs. Keller said.

"But we cannot punish her when she does not understand." Captain Keller shook his head. "If only we could find someone who could help her."

2. The Stranger

One morning soon afterward Helen woke early. She could not see the daylight, but she smelled bacon cooking. She knew it was time to get up. Her mother hurried Helen through breakfast and then dressed her.

Helen did not know what was happening. Still she felt excited. When her father lifted her into the carriage, she wondered where they were going.

Soon they were on a train. Helen did not understand the strange rumble of the wheels. But she could feel that they were moving. She could feel the train rocking and swaying. When the whistle blew, she could feel the vibration.

Helen's mother and father were taking her on a long trip to Baltimore, Maryland. They took her to a famous doctor who had helped many blind children.

After the doctor had tested Helen's eyes and ears, he shook his head. "Helen will always be blind and deaf," he told her parents, "but she is very intelligent. She can learn. Perhaps Dr. Alexander Graham Bell can help you find someone to teach her."

The Kellers went to Washington to see Dr. Bell. He was famous as the inventor of the telephone. He had spent many years working to help deaf people.

Helen did not know why they had taken another

Dr. Alexander Graham Bell helped the Kellers find a teacher for Helen and became a lifelong friend of the family.

trip. She did not know the kind man who held her on his knee. She touched his face and felt his gentle smile. He let Helen hold his watch against her cheek. She could feel it tick.

Dr. Bell told Captain Keller about a school for blind children in Boston, Massachusetts. It was called the Perkins Institute.

"There was a girl named Laura Bridgeman who was blind and deaf," Dr. Bell said. "Dr. Howe at the Perkins Institute taught her to understand words by spelling with his fingers. He pressed the letters against her hand and showed her how to make each letter of the alphabet with her own fingers. Dr. Howe is dead. You must write to Dr. Anagnos at Perkins. Ask him to find a teacher who will help Helen."

After the journey home to Alabama, Helen lived in the same dark world again. Her mind was like a wild bird in a cage. She still flew into terrible tempers. She did not know that her mother and father were hoping that Dr. Anagnos could send a teacher for her.

Many months passed. Then one spring day Helen felt excitement in the house again. All day she grew more curious. She waited on the front porch until at last she felt the thud of a horse's hooves in the drive. A carriage stopped. There was a thump as a heavy suitcase was set down.

Helen felt new footsteps coming toward her. Her

curiosity was bursting. She rushed at the stranger and felt a young woman's arms go around her. Helen's fingers flew over the new face and clothes and handbag.

The stranger had a nice, smiling face. She took Helen's hand and led her upstairs. Soon Helen was helping the stranger unpack. She found a doll. From the stranger's signs she understood that it was a present for her.

Helen hugged the doll. Then she felt the stranger take her hand and make queer signs in it with her fingers. Helen felt the same signs over and over. The stranger was making the letters that spelled *d-o-l-l*. She was showing Helen her very first word in the finger alphabet, but Helen did not understand. Helen was frightened. She threw the doll away and ran to find her mother.

The stranger was a young woman named Anne Sullivan. Dr. Anagnos had sent Anne from Perkins Institute in Boston. Anne had been a pupil in the school. She had been almost blind herself. But her blindness was not the same as Helen's. When she was sixteen, an operation helped her to see again.

Now Anne Sullivan was 21. Her eyes were still weak, but she had started to earn her living. She had come to Tuscumbia to be Helen Keller's teacher. Soon "Miss Annie" was a new member of the family.

3. W-a-t-e-r

The next weeks were an adventure for Helen. She liked the sewing cards and the kindergarten beads that Annie gave her. She liked their long walks through the cool woods. They rode horseback together. Annie led Helen's pony.

Whatever they did, Annie spelled letters into Helen's hand. When they petted the cat, Annie spelled *c-a-t*. Helen quickly learned to imitate Annie's fingers. She could make the letters for *c-a-k-e* when she wanted a treat, and *m-i-l-k* when she was thirsty.

"Helen is like a clever little monkey," Annie wrote. "She has learned the signs to ask for what she wants, but she has no idea that she is spelling words."

Helen enjoyed the adventures with Annie, but she did not know that the stranger was her teacher. She was very unhappy when Annie tried to make her obey.

Annie did not believe that Helen's parents were right to let Helen always do exactly as she pleased. At mealtimes Helen walked around the table. She dipped her fingers into everyone's plates and gobbled whatever she wanted.

Annie made Helen sit in her own chair and eat from her own plate. Helen was furious. When Annie gave her a spoon, Helen threw it on the floor and kicked the table. They spent a whole afternoon fighting while Annie insisted that Helen fold her napkin.

Mrs. Keller was upset. "I cannot bear to have Helen punished," she said.

Annie was firm. "We must make Helen know we love her," she said. "But we must not let her think she is different because she is blind and deaf. She must behave like other children."

Helen's bad tempers went on. Once she locked Annie in her room and hid the key. Captain Keller had to use a ladder to help Annie down.

One morning during her lesson, Helen was especially bad. She slammed her new doll on the floor and broke it. Annie was too tired to go on with the lesson. Her eyes ached. She took Helen by the hand and led her outdoors. They stopped at the pump for a drink.

Then something happened that changed Helen's whole life.

Helen held her hand under the spout while Annie pumped. As cold water poured over Helen's hand, Annie spelled in her other hand *w-a-t-e-r*. A new expression came into Helen's face. She spelled *water* several times herself. Then she pointed to the ground. Annie quickly spelled *g-r-o-u-n-d*.

Helen jumped up. She suddenly realized that she was understanding words. She pointed to Annie, and

Annie spelled *t-e-a-c-h-e-r*. Helen never called Annie by any other name.

Then Helen pointed to herself, and Annie slowly spelled out *H-e-l-e-n K-e-l-l-e-r*. Helen's face broke into a wide smile. It was the first time she knew that she had a name.

Helen and Annie were both excited. They raced to the house to find Mrs. Keller. Helen threw herself in her mother's arms while Annie spelled *m-o-t-h-e-r* into her hand. When Helen nodded to show that she understood, there were tears of happiness in Mrs. Keller's eyes.

All the rest of the day Helen ran about touching things, and Annie spelled the names. When she touched her little sister, Annie spelled *b-a-b-y*.

At supper Annie rubbed her fingers. "No wonder my hand is numb from spelling," she said, smiling at Captain Keller. "Helen is trying to make up in one day what other children have taken six years to learn."

When Helen went to bed that night, she kissed her teacher for the first time. Annie wrote, "I thought my heart would burst with joy."

Helen herself said many years later, "I was born again that day. I had been a little ghost in a 'no-world.' Now I knew my name. I was a person. I could understand people and make them understand me."

Helen Keller at the age of seven

4. Discoveries

Soon Helen could spell enough words to ask questions. She wanted to know what her mother and father and sister and teacher looked like. She learned that Annie had black hair and pretty blue eyes. Annie had a merry Irish wit, and she taught Helen to love laughter.

Helen's days were happy that summer. Every morning she and Annie had lessons. Annie made maps out of clay. Helen could feel the shapes of mountains and rivers and continents. Annie gave Helen an orange to hold when she explained that the world was round. When the lesson was over, Helen held up the orange and laughed. "Now we can eat the world," she spelled.

Helen learned to count with wooden beads and straws. She touched trees and flowers and learned their names. She held an egg in her hand and felt a baby chick peck its way out. She put her hand in a bowl of water and felt tadpoles swim between her fingers.

One morning there was a surprise for Helen. Annie gave her several square cards. On each card Helen could feel some raised dots. She was puzzled. Her fingers touched the dots carefully. Then Annie spelled the letter *a* with her fingers and put Helen's finger on a card. The raised dots on the card meant *a* also.

Helen soon began to understand. The dots were another way of spelling words.

This way of reading is called braille. It had been invented by a blind man named Louis Braille. The letters were printed in raised dots so blind people could read with their fingers.

For days Helen practiced reading the braille letters. When she knew them all, she put three cards together and spelled *d-o-g*. She ran to find Belle and made the dog's paws touch the letters.

One morning Helen spelled a whole sentence to surprise Annie. *D-o-l-l i-s o-n b-e-d*. Annie promised, "Tomorrow you shall have your first book in braille and start reading."

Helen had other important things to learn. She learned to dress herself neatly and make her own bed. She picked up her toys. She learned to be gentle with her little sister. She did not hit Belle or squeeze the kittens.

Sometimes Helen's old tempers came back. But when she touched Teacher's face and felt her mouth turn down, Helen knew she had been naughty. Helen's worst punishment was when Annie would not spell stories to her. Annie had taught Helen to love books as much as she did.

When Christmas came, Helen helped make spicy cookies. It was the first Christmas she had understood. She smelled the tree and helped trim its pine branches. Annie helped her wrap presents to surprise the family.

On Christmas night Captain and Mrs. Keller looked at Helen. She sat under the tree holding her new doll. Her face was full of love and joy and understanding.

Mrs. Keller took Annie's hand. "Miss Annie," she said, "I thank God every day of my life for sending you to us."

5. "I Can Speak!"

Just before Helen's eighth birthday, her mother and Teacher took her to Massachusetts. They visited Boston and the seashore at Cape Cod.

It was very different from Helen's last trip by train. Now she understood where they were going. She sat by the window and spelled questions about everything they passed. Annie spelled the answers into Helen's hand. Often she spelled out a joke, and they both laughed. They could spell back and forth almost as fast as other people could talk with their voices.

Helen had brought her favorite doll, Nancy, and some of her braille books. When her mother and Annie wanted to rest, Helen curled up with Nancy and read a story to herself. Once a friend asked Helen why she loved books so much.

"Because they tell me about things I cannot see," Helen answered. "And they are never tired or troubled like people."

At the seashore Helen could not wait to run to the beach. The sand was warm on her feet. She felt the roar and crash of the sea and jumped with excitement. Before Annie could stop her, she ran straight into a big wave. She tumbled head over heels and came out spluttering.

"*Who put salt in the water?*" Helen spelled. Her mother and Annie laughed. Soon Helen could jump through waves safely.

When summer ended, Mrs. Keller went home. Helen and Annie stayed in Boston. Dr. Anagnos had asked Helen to be a pupil at the Perkins Institute. Annie was still Helen's special teacher, but Helen had some lessons in classrooms. She made friends quickly with the blind children.

It was the first time Helen had friends her own age. They could spell to her and understand her fingers. Helen played dolls with the girls. She learned outdoor games. "London Bridge" and tag were her favorites. Helen loved to run fast.

There began to be stories in the newspapers about the little girl from Alabama. People were amazed that a deaf and blind child could read and understand words. Many teachers and important people came to visit Helen. Even Queen Victoria, across the sea in England, heard of her.

Annie was worried. "Helen is becoming a very famous little girl," she told Dr. Anagnos. "I am afraid that so much attention will spoil her."

Helen was too busy to know that anyone was worried. She was studying Latin and German and arithmetic. She discovered dozens of stories she could read in braille in the school library.

"Helen gobbles books like cookies," Dr. Anagnos smiled. "She cannot get enough." Helen began to write stories and poems herself.

When winter came, Helen helped the other children make a snow man. She loved coasting and tobogganing.

In Helen's second year at the Perkins Institute, she heard of a little blind-deaf boy named Tommy Stringer. He had no family.

"We must help," Helen spelled to Annie. They gave a party to raise money to help bring Tommy to the Perkins school. Helen was his special friend. When Tommy learned to spell his first words, Helen was proud of him.

When Helen was ten years old, she had a new hope. She heard that a blind-deaf girl in Norway had been taught to use her own voice and speak clearly. Helen wanted to learn to speak herself.

Miss Sarah Fuller gave Helen lessons. She was a teacher at the Horace Mann School for the Deaf in Boston. First Helen would put her hand on Miss Fuller's face when she talked. Then Helen would try to copy the way Miss Fuller's lips and tongue moved.

It was hard work. Over and over Helen tried to make the sounds of *M*, *P*, *S*, *A*, *T*, and the other letters. But she could not hear the sounds she made. She did not know when her voice sounded queer to others.

After each lesson, Helen practiced with Annie. At

Helen (left) was able to understand what Teacher said by touching Teacher's lips as she spoke.

last, one day, she could speak a whole sentence that Annie could understand. They were both overjoyed.

Helen was going home for vacation. She could not wait to show her family that she could truly speak. On the train to Alabama, she practiced saying, "Hello, father and mother. Hello, Mildred."

The family met Helen and Annie at the station. When they heard Helen speak, they hugged her with love and pride.

On the way home Helen planned one more surprise. At the front steps she jumped out of the carriage first.

"Come, Belle—" she called. When the old dog trotted up and licked her hand, Helen cried happily, "Now Belle can understand me too!"

6. College

The year Helen was fourteen, she went to the Wright-Humason School in New York. Annie sat beside Helen in classes. She spelled the teacher's words into Helen's hand.

Dr. Humason gave Helen special lessons in speaking and lip reading. She learned to put her fingers on other people's lips and understand what they were saying.

Helen made a new friend in New York. It was Mark Twain, the famous author of *Tom Sawyer* and

Huckleberry Finn. Mark Twain told Helen funny stories. He loved to make her laugh. "I lecture to thousands of people," he said, "but Helen is my best audience."

Helen had a serious plan to tell Mark Twain. She wanted to go to college. But first she must go to another school and study to prepare for college. It would mean long, hard work. The school would be expensive.

Helen explained to Mark Twain that her father was ill. "I cannot ask him for the extra money," she said.

Mark Twain encouraged Helen. He and some of her other friends raised money to help pay her school expenses.

"I will work hard," Helen promised. She studied at the Gilman School in Boston and with private teachers. She used a braille typewriter to keep her study notes. She learned to use a regular typewriter for her school papers.

Shortly before examination time, sad news came from Helen's home. Her father, Captain Keller, had died. It was hard for Helen to go on studying. She longed to go home and comfort her mother and sister. But she had to stay to take her exams.

Annie was not allowed to go into the examination room with Helen. A teacher spelled the questions into Helen's hand. Then Helen typed the answers.

The next week Helen heard that she had passed all her subjects. She would enter Radcliffe College in the fall of 1900. Now she could join her family and rest for the summer.

When college classes began, Annie sat next to Helen. Annie spelled what the teachers said into Helen's hand. Annie looked up words in the dictionary for Helen. She read Helen books that were not printed in braille.

The girls in Helen's class were friendly. They elected her vice-president of the class.

English was Helen's favorite subject. She wrote such good themes that some were published in a book. A magazine paid her to write the story of her life. Helen was glad she could earn money.

A young teacher named John Macy helped Helen with her writing. He was soon a friend of both Helen and Annie. They went boating together on the Charles River. They took picnic lunches and went hiking in the woods.

Helen's last year of college work was the hardest. Besides her studying, Helen now had Annie to worry about. Annie's delicate eyes were red and sore from all her reading to Helen. Helen begged Annie to rest, but Annie was firm. "I will not rest until you graduate," she told Helen.

John Macy came to the rescue. He helped Annie

read to Helen. Soon Helen realized that John was falling in love with Annie. She hoped that Annie would love John too.

In June of 1904, Helen was graduated from college with honors. Annie proudly watched Helen take her diploma.

7. A New Career

Helen and Annie went to live in Wrentham, near Boston. John Macy still came to see them often.

On one bright May afternoon, Helen stood beside Teacher as Annie and John Macy were married.

Helen was very happy about the marriage. Annie and John lived in Wrentham with her, and now the three planned to work together.

Helen had a hard time deciding what work would be best for her. "You should teach," many of her friends advised her.

Helen wanted to pass on the gift of teaching that Annie had given her. But at last she decided she could work best by writing and lecturing. "I can tell more people about the special training that deaf and blind children need," she told Annie. "I can teach them what you taught me—that children must not be different because they are blind or deaf. They can learn to work and be happy."

One memorable summer Alexander Graham Bell accompanied Annie, Helen, and Mrs. Keller on a trip to Niagara Falls.

Before she began to lecture, Helen took more voice lessons. She practiced for many hours so that people could understand her speeches.

During the next years, Helen and Annie lectured to big audiences all over the country. Traveling on trains and meeting thousands of strangers was hard work. But they were happy when they saw new schools being started and new organizations helping to educate the blind and deaf.

Between trips Helen wrote books and articles for magazines. After each long trip, she was happy to come home to Wrentham. She always went first to the garden and put her arms around her favorite trees. Her Great Dane dog and the puppies barked their welcome.

Helen and Annie rode horseback over the country trails. She and Annie and John spent long evenings by the fire with their friends.

Helen had always worked to get more books printed in braille. She knew that many blind people did not have enough books to read. She went to Washington to ask people in the government to help.

In 1913 there was important news. The National Library for the Blind was started. Helen and Annie went to Washington again. President Taft opened the new library.

Later Helen met President Taft again. He came to

New York to open the first Lighthouse for the Blind. Helen made a speech. She welcomed the new group that would work for the blind.

That night, when they had supper by the fire, Helen smiled.

"We started long ago with little Tommy Stringer," she told Annie. "We have traveled until our bones ached. We have talked ourselves hoarse to tell people that blind and deaf children need special schools. People have listened. Our dreams are coming true."

But a few years later, trouble came. Annie was ill. Her marriage with John Macy was not working out well, and the couple decided to separate. When John left Wrentham, Annie and Helen missed him sadly.

At the same time, Helen's work grew so heavy that she and Annie needed more help. A young Scottish girl named Polly Thompson came to live with them. Polly was quick and sensible and jolly. She could cook and give the dogs baths. She helped Helen with writing and reading to rest Annie's eyes.

Without John's help, the house in Wrentham was too expensive for Helen to keep. She was sad to leave the home she had loved. "We can take the dogs with us," she said. "But we will miss the garden."

They moved to a smaller house in Forest Hills, near New York City. Soon Helen was working hard on a new book.

8. War

In 1917 the United States entered World War I in Europe. The roar of faraway guns brought more changes to Helen Keller's life.

Helen had to give up many of her lecture trips. She and Teacher were very unhappy over the sad war news. They grieved for the many soldiers who were killed or wounded.

Shortly after the war ended, Helen was asked to act in a movie. It would tell the story of her life.

"A new adventure will be good for us," Helen said. She still needed more money to take care of herself and Annie and Polly. They traveled to California.

The movie work was exciting. In one scene Helen had to fly in an open plane. It did daring stunts. In another scene she rode a frisky horse that nearly threw her off. Annie and Polly gave Helen a new nickname. They called her "Daredevil Helen."

Soon afterward Helen and Annie were asked to do an act together on the stage. They were to appear in theaters all over the country.

They were both nervous the first time the curtain rolled up. The spotlights were bright. Annie came on the stage first and told about Helen's early life. When Helen came on, the audience always clapped.

Helen read Annie's lips and answered questions

Helen was well known to the American people during the First World War. She is seen in this picture christening a torpedo boat.

from the audience. Some of the questions were foolish.

"Do you shut your eyes when you go to sleep?"

"I never stayed awake to find out," Helen answered.

The act was a success. Helen and Annie earned the money they needed.

Now Helen could work again for others. She was happy with the news from Washington. Congress had voted money for many more books for the blind. Some could be played on records. They were called "talking books."

The American Foundation for the Blind was an active new group. Helen went to work for the foundation.

Helen Keller was famous around the world now. She had met people from every country. She had been invited to visit every president in the White House since her childhood.

But darkness was closing in again. Helen's mother had died, and Annie became very ill. The year was 1936. Annie was 70 years old. Her eyes were worn out with work. She was almost blind. But Annie had seen Helen succeed. She had seen new work for the blind beginning all over the country, much of it from Helen and Annie's work.

Annie was sick for many months. Helen sat beside her long nights. She and Polly nursed Annie tenderly.

Helen held Teacher's hand when she died. Helen felt as if her own life had ended. They had been together for almost 50 years. It was the saddest time of Helen's life. "A light has gone out that can never shine for me again," she said.

9. Around the World

Many people wrote Helen letters of sympathy. One from a stranger began: "I know, dear Helen Keller, your heart is crying out for the loved one. Our only comfort is to do what good we can in this world."

Helen was deeply touched. She felt as if Annie's own words were reaching her through the stranger's letter. "We must stop feeling sad and get back to work," she told Polly.

Soon afterward an important telegram came. The Japanese government asked Helen to help start work for their blind and deaf. This meant a long trip across the Pacific Ocean. It meant giving many speeches.

"I cannot say no," Helen said. "There are many thousands of deaf and blind children in Japan. We must help raise money to start schools for them, just as we are doing in America."

On the ship, crossing the ocean, Helen wrote the speeches she would give in Japan. She and Polly got up at five o'clock each morning to go out on deck alone. Then Helen would practice her speeches so Polly could tell her if her voice sounded right.

In Japan crowds greeted Helen. They threw flowers in front of her car. Best of all, Helen liked the children who gathered around to greet her.

When it was time to leave, Helen and Polly had raised enough money to begin the new schools. The Japanese government thanked them. The emperor of Japan sent a grateful message.

At home again Helen was busy. Her desk was piled high with letters to answer. Many parents who had blind or deaf children wrote to Helen for advice. She answered them all.

Helen was proud of the children she had helped.

Tommy Stringer, the blind-deaf boy, was now a tall, strong man. He earned his living as a carpenter. He had a family of his own.

One day a friend of Helen's came home from a walk. "I did not see anything interesting," she said. Helen was amazed. It made her think how much she wished she could see—even for a little while. Later she wrote a magazine article called "If I Had Three Days to See."

Helen wrote that first she would want to see the faces of her family and friends she loved. Then she wanted to see her house and her books and her dogs. She would go for a long walk through the woods. She wished that she could see a sunset, and children playing, and the moon and stars. She wanted to see a stage play and a funny movie.

While Helen worked, she thought of Teacher's empty room next to her study. It made her feel lonely again. Soon she and Polly moved to a new house in Westport, Connecticut.

The shadow of war was over the country again. Fighting had begun in Europe. America entered the war in 1941. Helen and Polly were sad that Japan was now America's enemy.

Many soldiers and sailors were blinded in the fighting. President Roosevelt asked Helen to visit them. She traveled to hospitals all over the country.

"You can learn to read and to work again," she told the men. "You must learn to be a part of the world and not outside of it." Her words and her gentle touch brought them new courage and hope.

10. Peace

In 1945 the long war ended. The next year Helen and Polly went to Europe to help the blind there.

One evening in Rome, Helen felt the quick excitement of Polly's hand. Polly was spelling terrible news. Their house in Westport had been burned. Everything was lost.

Worst of all, a book Helen had been writing about Teacher had been burned. It had been nearly finished. "The very first thing I will do is start the book over again," Helen said.

Back in Westport, Helen's loyal friends helped build a new house. The day Helen and Polly moved into their new home, huge boxes arrived. Helen's friends in Japan had sent gifts of tables and lamps and other furniture. The emperor had sent the most beautiful gift of all, a tall incense burner.

Many honors came to Helen Keller through the years. Colleges all over the world gave her special honors. Many foreign governments gave her medals.

Most important, Helen saw more and more blind

and deaf people educated to do useful work and be a part of the living world. Much of the help had come from her. Great countries, and little children, gave Helen their thanks.

In May 1959 Helen was given the honor she prized most. The Helen Keller World Crusade was begun at the United Nations building in New York City. It would help blind and deaf children all over the world.

Helen was very proud. She had lived through two terrible world wars. She had always hoped for world peace. Now it made her happy to know that people of different countries and races would work together to help children.

Helen Keller at her typewriter, near the end of a long and fruitful life.

Long after the time when most people retire, Helen Keller was busy. "I cannot stop to grow old while there is so much work to do," she said, "and so many children to help."

When Helen was 75, she traveled thousands of miles around the world. She made many speeches and met many new friends.

On her eightieth birthday the American Foundation for Overseas Blind announced the Helen Keller International Award. There is also a Helen Keller Scholarship for blind-deaf students.

Helen never forgot that all of her work and all of her honors and all the light in her life came first from her beloved Teacher. One of Helen Keller's most beautiful books is her story of Anne Sullivan Macy's life. She called the book simply *Teacher*.

When Helen Keller died in June 1968 she was 88 years old. At her funeral these words were spoken by Senator Lister Hill from the state of Alabama where Helen Keller was born:

> Her spirit will endure as long as man can read and stories can be told of the woman who showed the world that there are no boundaries to courage and faith.

JACQUELINE COCHRAN
1910–

Jacqueline Cochran stood toe to toe with men pilots and competed for speed records. She asked for no favors. She needed none. Jackie was used to facing challenges and winning. It took courage to climb into the cockpit of a jet airplane. It took courage, too, to overcome a loveless and deprived childhood. Until Jackie was eight years old she had no shoes. Her food was the barest minimum. Her dresses were usually cast-off flour sacks. But she believed in herself; and with hard work, intelligence, and persistence, Jackie Cochran became a nurse, millionaire businesswoman, and test pilot. Jackie's kind of courage is contagious. It proves to others who face overwhelming odds that like Jackie Cochran, they can make it on their own!

Jacqueline Cochran
First Lady of Flight

by Marquita O. Fisher

Copyright © 1973
by Marquita O. Fisher

1. The Girl Who Didn't Belong

Jacqueline Cochran laughed and patted the elephant's trunk. "Good boy," she said as she poured another bucketful of water into the tub for the big animal to drink. Some of it ran out onto her bare feet. Her dress, made from cotton flour sacks, was wet and streaked with mud. But she didn't mind.

Jackie was a skinny six-year-old, but she was determined to show the circus people she could do a good job. Then when they moved on in the morning, perhaps they would take her with them.

How wonderful that would be, she thought. The circus people had been jolly and kind. No one had screamed at her and beat her as mama did at home. There was plenty of food here too. Why, there was even some bread left over after dinner—a sight Jackie had never seen before. Yes, to go with the circus would be wonderful!

Jackie wondered if mama, papa, or her two older brothers and two older sisters had missed her yet. No, she decided, remembering when she was lost in the woods and no one had cared enough to look for her.

The elephant's tub was filled now. All the people

who had crowded the fairground earlier that evening had left for home. Most of the lamps were dark. Jackie curled up on a pile of straw near the elephant. She allowed herself only a moment to stare up at the summer sky filled with stars; then she closed her eyes. The circus would be leaving at dawn, and she wanted to get up early.

When morning came, Jackie awoke with a start and looked around. The fairground was empty. Jackie's brown eyes filled with tears. But she had learned long before that it did no good to cry. There was nothing to do now but go home.

In 1916 home for Jackie was a one-room shack in a poor mill town in northern Florida. It stood on wooden posts at the edge of a swamp. There were no window panes. Sometimes bats flew about in the attic, and bedbugs marched up and down the walls and floors. There was no electricity or running water. Jackie slept on the floor.

Jackie hated going back to the crowded little house, but she had nowhere else to go. She didn't want to face again the scoldings, the disorder, and the constant hunger.

"Why can't we live better?" she asked mama a few days later.

"Where do you think we'd get the money?" mama shouted, angered by the question. "The lumber mill doesn't pay papa and the boys enough to buy food, let alone fix this place up."

But Jackie knew that other people who were just as poor seemed to manage better. She wished mama would try to be more clean and orderly!

As the summer wore on, Jackie did her best to help find things to eat. Sometimes she caught fish or crabs. Often she would wait by a dock until a fisherman felt sorry for her. Then he might give her a mullet from his catch. Once she was so hungry that she stole a sweet potato from a farmer who was cooking a potful for his pigs.

Jackie often dreamed of escaping to faraway places where there would always be enough food, a warm bed, and shoes to wear when it was cold or raining.

Later that summer, when Jackie was sitting outside the house, mama's voice came through the window. "They left Jackie for us to bring up," she was saying to a visiting neighbor. "They made us promise we would never tell."

Jackie didn't wait to hear any more. She ran quickly away where no one could see her. Then she jumped up and down for joy.

"I'm glad I'm not one of them," she almost shouted.

Now she became even more determined to leave home. But until she could find a way, Jackie went back to school when it opened.

2. School Begins and Ends

Jackie had started school the year before, but on the third day the teacher tried to whip her with a ruler. Jackie struck back, then ran for the door. She didn't go back that year. But now a new teacher from Ohio had come to the little schoolhouse. Jackie decided to try school once again.

Jackie liked the beautifully dressed Miss Bostwick at once. She was strict with the children and made them work hard. She slapped them on their hands with a ruler when they misbehaved. But she was fair.

Two days after school began, the teacher took Jackie aside. "I'll pay you ten cents a week if you'll bring firewood to my room at the boardinghouse every day. Will you do it?" Jackie could hardly believe her good luck.

Right after school that day, Jackie got some wood and managed to climb the steps to the second floor. Miss Bostwick was waiting for her in the doorway.

Jackie's brown eyes widened in delight as she peeked over the armload of wood. She had never seen such a cozy room. A little stove glowed in the corner. Pretty pictures decorated the walls. Flowered curtains hung at the window. Jackie wanted to return again and again.

Each day she took Miss Bostwick several loads of

wood. Finally Miss Bostwick had to say, "Jackie, if you bring me any more firewood, I won't have room for my bed!"

Jackie and the teacher soon became good friends. After school, Jackie would go home with Miss Bostwick and sit spellbound while her teacher read books aloud by the hour. Jackie began to dream of the faraway places and interesting people Miss Bostwick read about.

During the next two years, Miss Bostwick spent many special hours with Jackie. Besides teaching her to love books, she taught Jackie to take pride in her appearance. Now every morning Jackie filled a tub with cold water from the pump and took a bath. Mama and her sisters laughed at her "foolish ways."

Miss Bostwick also gave Jackie a comb and ribbon and showed her how to fix her long, dark-blonde hair. She bought Jackie a new dress—the first ready-made dress she had ever owned. Jackie no longer felt ashamed of the way she looked in school or anywhere she went.

Although no one else in the family went to church, mama sent Jackie once a month when the priest came to town. Jackie wondered if it was because of a promise made to her real parents.

The priest, like Miss Bostwick, became Jackie's friend. Both seemed to be telling her, "You can rise above all this. Study, work hard, find the stars." With their help, Jackie became happier and continued to learn each day.

But Jackie's happy times did not last long. At the close of her second year of school, Miss Bostwick told her gently, "I'm going to move back to Ohio."

Jackie's heart filled with sadness. For her no other teacher could ever take Miss Bostwick's place. She continued to study and read, but she never again went back to school.

3. Jackie Finds Work

That fall the wife of a mill worker asked, "Jackie, would you help me take care of the house and kids until our new baby comes? I'll pay you ten cents a day."

Jackie, who was now about eight years old, eagerly accepted the job. She did the housework and watched the children. She even cooked the meals, although she had to stand on a box to reach the stove.

Soon other people nearby heard that Jackie was a good worker. She was hired by one family after another. One time she even delivered a baby because there was no doctor or neighbor to help.

December came, and Jackie saw a beautiful doll in the window of the general store. She longed for it with all her heart.

"It's not for sale," the storekeeper told her. "Each time you spend 25 cents here, I'll put a slip of paper with your name on it in this bowl. The person whose name I draw on Christmas Eve wins the doll."

Jackie had earned four dollars, but no one had the money to pay her yet. So Jackie found other jobs to do. She drew well water, scrubbed clothes, and worked until her hands bled. When she had saved 50 cents, she ran to the store.

"I want two chances on the doll," she said breathlessly. She bought 50 cents' worth of presents for her sisters and for Willy Mae, the two-year-old baby of the oldest sister. But the important thing to Jackie was that she had a chance to win.

Early Christmas Eve Jackie hurried to the store for the drawing. She was standing right beside the storekeeper when he pulled the slip of paper from the bowl. He paused, lowered his glasses, and read, "Jacqueline." The doll was hers!

Jackie flew home with the prize clutched in her arms. She flung open the door and held the doll up for the family to see. Mama turned away from the stove and frowned. "You're too big for that," she said. Papa grabbed the beautiful doll and gave it to Willy Mae. It was all Jackie could do to hold back the tears.

The Christmas season passed, and a few weeks later the sawmill closed down. It was time to move on.

People were saying that the cotton mills in Columbus, Georgia, needed workers. So the family picked up what few belongings they could carry and walked three miles to the railroad station. They climbed into a caboose for a free ride on the next train to Georgia.

Finally they reached Columbus. What luck! The mills were humming day and night. Even eight-year-old Jackie got a job and was promised six cents an hour. She would work from six o'clock in the evening until six o'clock in the morning and would be off all day Sunday.

Jackie had never been happier!

4. Jackie Learns a Trade

Jackie's job at the mill was to deliver huge bobbins of thread to the weavers. All through the night she pushed a heavy cart from one noisy loom to another. Lint hung in the air like fog and made her cough. Her bare feet ached. There was no place to sit down, even during the half-hour lunch break. But Jackie was earning money, so she did not complain.

At the end of the first week of work, Jackie eagerly waited in line to collect her $4.50 paycheck. Pictures of all she might buy raced through her mind. But when she got home, mama took the money away from her. The next week, Jackie gave mama only three dollars and kept a dollar and a half for herself. Then she went to a street peddler.

"I want some shoes," she told him.

The peddler reached for some plain brown ones.

"Oh, no," she said and pointed to a pair of high-heeled shoes—the kind she had seen well-dressed women wear on the street. "I want those."

The peddler smiled. Her feet, like her hands, were large for a little girl. Still he had to search the cart for his smallest pair of high-heeled shoes. Jackie paid him, put on the shoes, and stumbled proudly away. They were the first shoes she had ever owned.

Before Jackie was ten, she was put in charge of

When Jackie was a little girl, children were often hired to work the machinery in cotton mills.

about fifteen other children. She and her family worked very hard to buy enough to eat and to pay the rent. They suffered in the heat of summer when the mill was hot and stuffy. In the winter, chilly air seeped through the cracks in the walls, and the workers were cold.

While they worked, Jackie talked with the other girls.

"Someday I'm going to be rich," she told them. "I'm going to own a big car and pretty clothes and travel all over the world."

Her friends laughed at Jackie's dream. The world of comfort and excitement seemed too far away.

Finally the people at the mill decided to ask the mill owners to make working conditions better and to pay the workers more money. When the mill owners refused to do these things, the workers went on strike and left their jobs. Jackie walked off with the others.

Weeks passed, and still the mill owners would not make any changes. The workers still refused to go back to their jobs. They had no money left for rent or food.

Then one day Jackie heard that a woman named Mrs. Richler needed someone to help her at home and in her beauty shops. Jackie went at once to the Richlers' house. A dark-haired woman answered the door.

"I'd like a job," Jackie said at once. She didn't want to give the woman a chance to say no, so she kept talking. "I can cook real good. I'll work hard. Look how big my hands are. I can learn real fast and . . ."

Mrs. Richler smiled at the spunky girl and said, "Anyone who can do so much at such an early age should be given a chance. Come in, my dear. I'd like you to meet my family."

Jackie stepped into the nicest house she had ever been in. Mrs. Richler introduced her to Mr. Richler and their six children. Jackie could tell at once they would be kind to her. When Mrs. Richler offered her $1.50 a week plus her room and meals, she quickly accepted.

Every weekday morning at five o'clock, Jackie got up to help with the breakfast and house cleaning. Then she went to one of the Richler beauty shops where she cleaned the floor and sinks and mixed bottles of shampoo and hair dyes. At night Jackie helped fix dinner and wash dishes.

A few months later the workers went back to the mill even though the company had made no changes. But Jackie stayed on with the Richlers.

Mrs. Richler followed the teachings of the Jewish religion faithfully. She taught Jackie what was right and what was wrong just as she taught her own daughters. Jackie soon felt like one of the family.

Jackie quickly learned the skills needed to become a beauty operator. By the time she was thirteen, she could operate the permanent-wave machine, a new invention. Now she was earning $35 a week.

She found out that mama and papa were even worse off than before. Jackie was old enough now to understand how hard it was for mama to run a household with so little money. Each week she gave mama some of her pay. Jackie saved most of the rest. By the time she was fourteen, she had saved several hundred dollars.

Then one morning, while Jackie was inside a booth waving a customer's hair, she overheard a salesman talking to Mrs. Richler.

"A shop in Montgomery would buy one of my permanent-wave machines if they could find an expert operator," he said. "Do you know of one?"

Jackie thought quickly. She could operate a permanent-wave machine as well as anyone, better than most. She pulled the curtain of the booth aside.

"I'm the expert you're looking for," she said. She did not mention her age.

Within a few days she had said a fond good-bye to the Richlers and her friends. She promised to keep sending money to her family.

Jackie was on her way to a new life in Montgomery, Alabama.

5. Out on Her Own

Jackie settled quickly into a cozy rented room and went to work in the department store beauty shop. One of the customers, Mrs. Lerton, was a judge in the Juvenile Court. She liked Jackie and became almost like a mother to her. She taught her how to sew her own clothes and do needlework. She helped her to meet nice young people. Soon Jackie was going to lots of parties. She and her friends had fun driving around in the Model T Ford she bought with some of her savings.

One day Mrs. Lerton was watching Jackie's quick but gentle movements as she worked on a customer. "You are so clever with your hands, Jackie," she said, "and you do like to help other people. Did you ever think about becoming a nurse?"

For the next several weeks, Jackie thought about what Mrs. Lerton had said. Jackie had been working in the beauty shop for two years now. She liked the work there, but she decided that nursing would enable her to help more people. "Yes," Jackie decided, "I will become a nurse."

Mrs. Lerton helped her to make the arrangements, and soon Jackie moved into the hospital and began her studies. As always, Jackie worked hard and learned quickly. She took a real interest in all the patients.

Even on her days off, she went into the wards to shave and cut hair for the people who were unable to help themselves.

When Jackie finished the three years of training, she moved to a small mill town in Florida, where she became the nurse for a poor, busy doctor.

One day Jackie and the doctor were called to a lumber camp for an emergency. They rode on a logging train about fifteen miles into the woods. As they walked toward the camp, they could hear a man moaning.

"His leg is crushed," a logger explained as he led them to the clearing where the man lay on the ground.

While the doctor examined the leg, Jackie asked the men to build a fire and heat a tubful of water. When the water was boiling, she put the doctor's instruments into it, including the saw they had brought along. The man's leg would have to be cut off.

Jackie and the doctor worked quickly. When the operation was finished, there was nothing more the doctor could do. He went back home, but Jackie stayed at the camp to take care of the patient. At night she slept in a chair while a logger kept watch. Every four hours she would be awakened to change the patient's bandages. A few days later, when Jackie was sure he would live, she returned home.

Jackie had taken this job because she remembered her life in Florida, and she knew how much the poor people needed help. They had no money to pay for the food and housing they needed. They had never been taught the importance of being clean.

One night Jackie sat alone caring for a sick woman. As the hours went by, she thought about her work. She began to see that she alone would never have the time, energy, or money to make a real difference in the lives of all those who needed help. By morning she decided that being a nurse no longer satisfied her.

"I will need money to help people," she told herself. "I have to go somewhere and find a way to earn it."

For the next two years, Jackie tried one job after another. She liked driving around the country selling various products. She liked working in beauty shops.

When Jackie was about twenty, she took a job at Antoine's, an expensive beauty salon in New York City. During the winter months she worked at Antoine's salon in Florida. Her list of happy customers grew, and so did her bank account.

After work, life was exciting and fun for the pretty girl with the long, blonde hair. She loved parties and dancing, and won several ballroom dancing contests. During quiet times she became so skilled at needlework that one sample took a prize at a country fair.

One night at a dinner party in Florida, Jackie was seated next to a slender, handsome man. She didn't know he was a very rich businessman.

Jackie's new friend, industrialist Floyd Odlum. Their chance meeting was to change the course of Jackie's life.

"I'm Floyd Odlum," he told her, introducing himself.

Jackie liked his quiet manner and warm sense of humor. She hoped she would see him again. He seemed to like her too.

As they talked, she told Floyd, "I'd like to work for a cosmetic company that has stores selling beauty aids across the country. It would be fun to travel from store to store and help to build business."

"You would need wings to do all that!" He laughed.

Wings! The idea of flying caught her imagination. She began to picture herself in the cockpit of a plane, flying from one business meeting to another.

But Jackie was still in Florida, and she had to be at work early the next morning. She left the party before midnight, knowing that both flying and Floyd Odlum would become important in her life.

6. Jackie Gets Her Wings

On the first morning of her three-week vacation, Jackie went to an airfield near New York City for her first flying lesson. "Husky," the pilot, showed her how to control the movements of the airplane with the stick and rudder pedals. He explained how the throttle controls the power of the engine. Jackie was eager to learn, so she listened carefully.

It was time for takeoff. Jackie held her breath. The plane roared down the runway and lifted. Jackie's heart began to pound with excitement. She knew then that she was going to become an aviator.

When they landed again, Husky explained what she had to do before she could get a pilot's license. "It usually takes two or three months," he added.

Jackie gasped. "I have only three weeks."

The big pilot laughed. "You'll never do it!" he said.

But Jackie spent every moment she could learning to fly. Only two days after the first flight, Jackie landed the old Fleet trainer, and Husky climbed out. "It's all yours," he said, closing the door behind him.

Jackie, alone in the plane, shivered with delight. She pushed the throttle in and headed down the hard dirt runway. In a few moments the wheels left the ground, and Jackie was on her first solo flight. The roar of the engine was one of the loveliest sounds she had ever heard. She felt as light as the fluffy cloud floating nearby.

Then suddenly the engine stopped. The only sound was the whooshing of the wind as the plane moved through the still air like a paper glider. The plane slowed down. If it did not stay at a certain speed, Jackie knew it would stop gliding and go into a deadly spin. Her hands tightened on the stick. "Don't panic," she told herself. "Think!" She remembered what she had learned and pushed the stick forward. The nose dropped down. The plane picked up speed.

Jackie looked down and nervously searched for the field. Hooray! The airstrip was close enough to glide down to. She sighed with relief. Then she directed the powerless plane toward the runway. Her first solo flight ended with what pilots call a dead-stick landing!

Floyd Odlum was now back in New York City. When Jackie told him what had happened, he laughed. "If you did that well on your first solo, you can surely earn a license in three weeks."

The men at the field, too, began rooting for her.

They liked the careful way the pretty 22-year-old girl examined the engine and didn't make a fuss when she got grease on her hands. They admired the way her bright, dark eyes studied the charts and heavy textbooks. They were amazed that she could look at a page and later see it in her mind almost like a picture.

Before the three weeks were up, Jackie was able to tell Floyd, "I did it! I have my private pilot's license." How happy he was for her!

In 1932 there were few women pilots, and Jackie was determined to be a good one. But this would take time. Jackie thought over the idea of starting her own cosmetic business. "Then I can plan my day so I can spend more time flying," she said. She was glad she had saved enough money to do this.

During the next two years, Jackie was very busy. She flew all over the country getting her new business under way.

At the same time she became a more skilled pilot. She learned to find directions by the positions of the stars. At that time, airplane radios carried messages only in the dots and dashes of Morse code. She mastered that too. Jackie learned how different kinds of airplane engines worked and how they could be repaired. She practiced flying blind, using the plane's instruments to find her way in bad weather. She became the first woman to make a completely blind landing.

By 1934 Jackie was a skilled pilot, and her business was doing well. She was ready for a new challenge; so she decided to enter her first air race. A friend, Wesley Smith, agreed to be her copilot.

Most of the planes flown in air races were loaned to pilots by the manufacturers. Thus new equipment could be tested. The manufacturers hoped that their planes would win, because more people would then choose their models.

The prize money was $50,000, and Jackie hoped to claim part of it. But she wasn't thinking of herself alone. There were others to care for.

Papa had died, but mama and others in the family still depended on her support. Willy Mae was now grown with a little daughter of her own. Jackie paid for them to go where Willy Mae could find a better job. In return for that help, Jackie told Willy Mae that she wanted back the doll she had won that Christmas Eve so many years before. "I don't believe anyone should get something for nothing," Jackie said.

The race Jackie and Wesley entered was to begin in London, England, and end in Melbourne, Australia. The little Gee Bee plane they planned to fly was not quite finished. They took it to England by ship, and mechanics worked on it all the way across the ocean.

Two days before the race, Jackie and Wesley climbed into the plane to fly it for the first time. One of the seats had not been put in yet, so Jackie had to sit on a big wooden cracker box. As soon as the two pilots took off, they could tell the plane was not as safe to fly as they could have wished.

When they came in for a landing, the plane hit the ground so hard that Jackie thought they'd broken a wing!

But when they checked the plane for damage, they found none. They learned that the plane always landed like that!

At dawn on the morning of the race, the planes from many different countries were lined up on the runway. Jackie and Wesley taxied the Gee Bee into position. They would be the seventh plane to take off.

Jackie looked out through the canopy at the thousands of people who had waited through the night to watch. "They seem almost as excited as I am," she thought.

Now it was time for the Gee Bee to take off. The crowd strained to watch as it raced down the runway. They could tell the pilots were having some trouble getting off the ground. The engine didn't seem to have enough power, but the plane rose at last, cleared the field safely, and climbed into the bright sunrise.

Jackie and Wesley breathed easier. They began to think that they might reach the first refueling stop in Bucharest, Rumania, ahead of the others.

7. Flying Firsts

From the start, the two pilots worried about the troublesome engine. Then, while flying over the snow-capped Carpathian Mountains in eastern Europe, they saw that the needle on the gas gauge for one tank pointed to empty. Jackie pulled a switch so that the engine would get its fuel from the full tank. But the engine sputtered and stopped. Wesley Smith opened his canopy and got ready to jump. He waited for Jackie. She reached for her canopy. It was stuck. "I can't get out of the plane!" she gasped.

The plane glided closer and closer to the mountaintops. Jackie twisted one fuel-line switch, then the other. Suddenly the roar of the engine sounded again. The pilots exchanged happy smiles. Then Jackie saw what had happened. She wrote a note and handed it to Wesley, since she could not make herself heard over the engine noise. The note said, "When the switch says ON, it means OFF. When it says OFF, it means ON."

But that was not the end of their troubles. As they came in for the landing at Bucharest, one wing flap became stuck. The other moved only a little. The plane was thrown out of balance. They climbed, went around the field, and tried again to land. The flaps stuck again. Jackie struggled to loosen her canopy and finally succeeded. They made signs to each other: "We'll have to jump if we don't make it this time."

At last they managed to get both flaps in up position. The plane touched down on the runway fast.

Jackie and Wesley knew the plane was not safe enough to continue in the race. They were bitterly disappointed.

When Jackie talked it over with Floyd later, he told her he hoped she would continue racing. The following year, she decided to enter one of the biggest and most important races in the United States—the Bendix Transcontinental Air Race. The pilots were to start in Los Angeles, California, and finish in Cleveland, Ohio.

The winner would receive a prize of several thousand dollars. But to Jackie, as to most pilots, racing was more than a chance to win fame and fortune. It was an opportunity to contribute more information about the science of flight.

When Jackie tried to sign up for the race, she was told, "Sorry, this race is not for women." Jackie would not accept that. She went to each man who was to fly in the Bendix and asked him to sign a paper which said he did not object to her racing. Only after every man agreed was she permitted to enter.

A few days before the race, Jackie noticed that the engine of the plane she was going to fly no longer ran smoothly and evenly. A man from the company that had provided the plane asked her to withdraw from the race. She refused. She could not back out now.

On the night of the takeoff from Los Angeles, fog rolled in so that the end of the runway could not be seen. The plane ahead of Jackie's roared down the runway. Suddenly there was a crash, and the plane burst into flames. The pilot, who was a friend of Jackie's, was killed. Jackie sat in her plane feeling sick with shock and sorrow. Photographers gathered around to snap her picture. They asked if she was still going to fly.

A man from the company that owned her plane ran onto the field. "Call off the flight," he begged her again.

Jackie left the plane to telephone Floyd. "What should I do?" she asked when she got through to him.

They talked about the choices she could make. But he left the decision to her.

Jackie was not afraid of dying. She had a strong belief that a person's spirit lives on after death. She was certain that death came only when it was time to die, and not before. Yet she wondered if her strong desire to enter the race was making her overlook its real dangers. After considering the possibilities carefully, she decided to stay in the race.

Jackie would use her instruments to make a blind takeoff into the wall of fog. A fire truck and an ambulance stood by. As she started down the runway, the engine of her plane did not put out the power she expected. But trying to stop would have meant crashing into the fence at the end of the runway. So with a prayer in her heart, Jackie pushed the engine to its limit. She caught her breath as she felt the wheels leave the ground.

But Jackie's plane was so low her radio antenna caught on the fence, and it was pulled off. She had no radio, but she was airborne. The engine shook. It overheated. Still Jackie flew eastward.

At dawn, she could see the Grand Canyon ahead. But she could also see what pilots feared most—an electrical storm. As she approached the storm, Jackie had to make an important decision. Should she risk flying her overheated plane through the strong winds, rain, and lightning or should she turn back? She wanted to continue. Good sense told her to go back. Full of disappointment she turned the plane and headed for the nearest airport.

The race was lost, but Jackie knew that she had won something—the Bendix would never again be closed to women.

8. A Bride Becomes a Winner

A few months later, on a lovely day in May of 1936, Jacqueline Cochran said, "I do," to Floyd B. Odlum. Jackie glowed with happiness.

"Floyd is at the center of everything Jackie does," a friend remarked, "and she is interested in everything he does."

Floyd encouraged Jackie to continue flying. Encouragement was what she needed. Several times she had nearly lost her life in flying accidents. She again entered the Bendix Race in 1937 and was disappointed when she came in third.

"It's the number on your plane," many people warned her. Jackie looked at the number 13 and laughed. Superstitions were a part of her. She felt certain that number 13 would someday bring her good luck.

Then, in 1938, she entered the Bendix Race for the third time.

It was about three o'clock in the morning when she climbed into the crowded cockpit of a little Seversky pursuit plane. She checked the oxygen tube and the

1937

1938

1938

Jacqueline Cochran: Record Setter

1937	Accepting the trophy for a new women's speed record.
1938	The takeoff. A third try at winning the Bendix.
1938	Winner of the 1938 Bendix Air Race!
1939	The end of a record-setting flight from Burbank to San Mateo and back at 309 miles per hour.

1939

radio. A soda bottle, half-filled with water, was propped nearby. It held a glass tube so she could sip the water without taking off her oxygen mask. She kept a few lollipops handy, too, to help keep her mouth moist.

Her maps, or charts, had been marked many weeks earlier when she first began to plan and train for the flight. Now she attached them to a string, then tied one end of the string to her leg. If the charts should get tossed off her lap during "bumpy" weather, she would be able to pull them back.

Trouble rode with her in this race too. She ran into bad weather. The gas tank in the right wing became blocked. The fuel would flow only when she tipped the plane.

But when the wheels of her plane touched the ground in Cleveland the next afternoon, she knew she had won first place. Two hundred thousand people stood and cheered.

A judge rushed to the runway to lead her to the winner's platform. He found her combing her hair and fixing her makeup.

"Where is my husband?" was her first question. She pushed through the cheering crowd. In a few minutes, she and Floyd were together. She clutched his arm. "I'm not afraid to fly cross-country," she said, "but in a crowd like this, I'm afraid without you!"

With each passing year, Jackie's life became more like her little-girl dreams come true. Jackie's cosmetic company did well, and Floyd continued to be successful. Among their friends were kings and presidents.

The girl who had once lived in a shack was now the owner of a new airplane and the mistress of three homes. Her favorite house was on a 600-acre date farm in the California desert. She and Floyd spent most of their time there.

But Jackie didn't forget what it was like to be poor. Neither did Floyd. The son of a small-town minister, he had also known difficult times during his childhood and had worked to pay his way through college. So Floyd nodded encouragement when Jackie told him she wanted to help the needy. Sometimes in her travels when she saw a child who was poor and uncared for, she checked into the family life and made arrangements at once for help. She also saw to it that dozens of children had the chance to go to school.

When Jackie wasn't with Floyd or managing her business, she was flying. She entered many more races, testing many new products. She tried out new engines, fuels, instruments, and propellers. She tested helmets, masks, and spark plugs. Some of these failed to work, and several times Jackie was nearly killed. But each test provided information, so the product could be made safer.

"What has been the greatest satisfaction you've had from flying?" Jackie was often asked.

"The testing I've done and the information developed from it," she would answer.

During this exciting time in her life, Hitler came to power in Germany and was trying to take over much of the world. Other countries in Europe had risen against him, and World War II was raging. Jackie often said to Floyd, "I wish I could do something to help in the war effort." Floyd was already busy helping the president improve the economy.

One day at a luncheon in Washington, D.C., Jackie talked with the chief of the Army Air Corps, General H.H. "Hap" Arnold. He told her about the men who were flying American planes from Canada to England for the use of the British air force. Then to her surprise General Arnold said, "Why don't you fly one of the bombers over to England? We need every plane we can get over there, and besides that, your flying would call attention to the need."

It was the kind of job Jackie had been hoping to find.

9. Jackie Goes to England

Jackie could not have guessed that most of the American pilots would be opposed to a woman flying bombers to Great Britain. One man took equipment out of the cockpit to keep her from being tested for the first flight. Others threatened to go on strike if she flew the plane. But finally they reached an agreement. Jackie would be listed as first officer and fly the plane. Captain Carlisle, a navigator who was also a fine pilot, would take the plane off the ground and land it.

At last everything was ready. Captain Carlisle took off at dusk, then turned the controls over to Jackie. Captain Carlisle went to his table and stayed there charting their position. The radio operator sat in his tiny room behind the pilot's cabin. Jackie handled the huge plane easily, following every rule in the book which she had studied carefully.

After a few hours, Jackie looked out in delight. There were the northern lights! But clouds hid the ocean from view as the plane raced on through the night. She and the crew ate sandwiches and hard-boiled eggs and drank tomato juice.

Then, just before daybreak, tracer bullets shot up around them through the darkness.

Captain Carlisle rushed forward. "Maybe they spotted us on radar," he said.

"Maybe it's one of our ships, and they think we're an enemy plane," Jackie suggested.

The radio operator came running out of his room

with his signal pistol. He opened the hatch and fired a flare that glowed the color that was the signal for the day. They hoped the bullets were coming from a friendly ship that would understand the signal and stop firing. But none of them really thought that the ship would be able to see the flare through the clouds.

Jackie flew straight ahead, getting out of the danger area as quickly as possible. They checked the plane and were happy to find there was no damage.

Soon after daybreak, Jackie caught sight of the coast of Ireland and began to follow a difficult air route. First she directed the plane one way, then the other, as written in her orders. The route was changed each day to make it impossible for enemy planes or submarines to figure out which way the Allied planes would fly.

Twelve hours after takeoff, they arrived in Scotland. It had been a night Jackie would never forget.

Reporters rushed up to the pretty American flier after the bomber landed. "How about some pictures, Jackie?" they begged.

Jackie shook her head. "These slacks need pressing. I can't be photographed in them."

The reporters laughed and waited until Jackie changed into a pretty dress. Then she posed for pictures. Writers everywhere called her "the glamour girl of aviation."

Jackie flew airplanes in wartime England as a captain in the British Air Transport Auxiliary.

After a short stay in England, Jackie returned to the United States.

The next morning at nine o'clock, she received the message that President Roosevelt wished her to be at Hyde Park for lunch that day.

"You're joking," Jackie said, but soon she realized it was no joke. A police escort rushed her by car to the president's home.

After lunch, she and the president went into his office. "Tell me what's going on in England—through a pilot's eyes," he asked her.

She told him about all she had seen and heard. They talked for nearly two hours.

Several days later, she was called into General Arnold's office.

"An English official has asked me if you would organize a group of American women pilots and take them to England," he told her.

Jackie had seen for herself how much England needed experienced pilots. Still, she hesitated.

"We'll be in this war someday too," she said at last. "I'm certain of that. Then all our pilots will be needed here."

"Yes, but the time has not yet come for that," General Arnold answered. "In the meantime, I hope you will accept the job in England. Learn what you can from the experience. Someday we'll need you to organize women pilots here."

Jackie talked with Floyd before deciding to take the job. They agreed that winning the war came before anything else. Both would work toward that end. Their life together would have to wait until the world was once again at peace.

Jackie began flying all over the country searching for experienced women pilots who were willing to fly for England. Twenty-five were finally chosen and trained. They were sent to England, with Jackie in charge as flight captain.

Jackie, like the rest of the women, mastered the dangerous task of flying planes in wartime England. The women flew planes from factories to airports and from one airport to another. They transported people and equipment. Each job they did freed a British pilot for combat work.

Soon after the United States entered the war, a brief message came from General "Hap" Arnold. "Come home," it said. Jackie went back to Washington as quickly as possible.

10. Women's Air Force Service Pilots

General Arnold asked Jackie to begin at once to find women pilots and to organize a training program for them. She chose Houston, Texas, as the base where the women would be trained. Letters from women fliers began to flow in. Jackie flew from city to city to interview each pilot personally. At last she chose 25 who, she felt, would set a fine example for other women pilots. They met at the field in Houston.

Jackie looked over the different kinds of old training planes collected for their use. She knew it would be useless to try to get better ones, for there was a wartime shortage.

Jackie took charge of the training program, and after several months of hard work, the first class of

Jackie pins the wings of a military pilot on a WASP at the first graduation. Members of the new unit (above) take part in maneuvers.

25 pilots was ready to graduate. But several days before graduation, Jackie became very sick. The doctor ordered her to stay in bed at the Cochran-Odlum Ranch in California. But Jackie was determined to go to Houston to take part in the graduation.

"It's 200 miles from here to the Phoenix Airport," her doctor reminded her. "You can't sit up that long in a car."

Jackie thought and thought. Finally she had an idea. She picked up the telephone and called the local undertaker.

"I would like to hire a hearse to drive me to Phoenix," she told him.

A few hours later, the long black car pulled up at Phoenix Airport. Jackie climbed out of the back and boarded the plane for Houston.

It was a shining moment for Jackie when she handed each member of that first graduation class a diploma.

As soon as Jackie grew well again, she returned to her post as director of the WASP—the Women's Air Force Service Pilots.

Jackie's scars from a much earlier operation were giving her a great deal of trouble and pain. Sometimes she was barely able to stand up. An air force doctor showed her how to stop the pain for a short time, but he also gave her a list of hospitals.

"Never be any farther than four hours' flying time

from any of these hospitals," he warned her. "You might need emergency treatment at any moment."

Yet Jackie kept busy day and night running the program. She even helped design the uniform the girls wore—a bright blue suit with army air force wings pinned to the jacket. While flying, they wore fur-lined overalls and boots, and a parachute.

It was not long before dozens of small groups of women fliers were working at different fields where Jackie had set up programs. During the first week of work at a field in North Carolina, two planes crashed, killing two women pilots. Saddened and shocked, Jackie flew at once to the field. The other women pilots were afraid. Some found excuses not to fly.

"The planes aren't safe," they told her.

Jackie took every plane up for a long, hard test ride. Each had at least one thing wrong with it.

"But what plane in wartime hasn't something wrong?" she asked the pilots. "These are as safe to fly as any."

The women returned to their work, but a few days later another plane crashed. The pilot was rushed to the hospital with a skull fracture.

Jackie was determined to find the cause for the crashes. Finally the report came through—sugar was found in the gasoline, and sugar in gasoline would stop the engine in a very short time. An enemy agent had been at work!

Doing what she could to win the war was Jackie's main concern. When she heard from the White House that many of the products she had tested were now being used by the air force, she glowed with pleasure. But there was no time to sit back and smile over past accomplishments. Directing the WASPs kept her busy day and night.

Before the war ended in 1945, more than 1,800 women had entered the training course. More than 1,000 of them graduated and flew with the air forces.

At the end of the war, Jackie received the Distinguished Service Medal for her special part in the war effort.

11. Breaking the Sound Barrier

In the years following the war, Jackie traveled all over the world, often with Floyd. She managed their homes well and made certain that food and money were not wasted. She spent many hours reorganizing her cosmetic business. She had had no time to oversee it during the war, and it was losing money. She also developed a new interest in politics, but flying was still first among the things she liked to do. She continued to test planes and enter races.

Jackie had only to look up at the growing number of jet trails tracking the sky to see that jets would be the aircraft of the future. "I'm not going to be left out of that part of aviation," she promised herself.

Because of her experience in high-speed flying, Jackie became a flight consultant, or adviser, in 1952 for a Canadian company that built the Sabre Jet F-86. Part of Jackie's job was to make speed tests at Edwards Air Force Base in California, where the weather was good and a speed course for timing was already set up. The company hoped that with the plane's new engine, she would break a woman's record or two and bring more business to the Canadian company. Jackie agreed, although she was only interested in breaking men's records.

Jackie went into strict training for the test flights. She went to bed early each night so that she would be well rested. She controlled her diet and exercised so that her body would be strong and healthy.

Jackie worked hard. She studied each part of the engine. "What does this valve do?" she asked one mechanic. "What does such high speed do to the fuel lines?" she asked another flier.

Colonel Charles "Chuck" Yeager was the first person to fly faster than the speed of sound and live to tell about it. He helped her in every way he could.

During Jackie's third flight in the Canadian Sabre Jet, Chuck Yeager flew in a jet nearby as an observer. Only he knew what she planned to do that day.

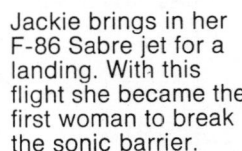

Jackie brings in her F-86 Sabre jet for a landing. With this flight she became the first woman to break the sonic barrier.

Jackie flew her jet plane higher and higher. As she rose, the sky around her became a darker blue. The sun was like a burning ball, but there was no sunlight as we know it here on earth. There, on the edge of space, she looked up and saw the stars. It was still midday.

Jackie kept the plane flying upward until it reached 45,000 feet, nearly 9 miles above the earth. Then, after moving the plane into the proper position, she pointed the nose of the Sabre Jet straight toward the ground and began her full power dive. She hoped to pass safely through the speed zone where dangerous shock waves build up. She was going to fly faster than the speed of sound! Many experienced pilots had tried to do this and had failed. She hoped to be the first woman to succeed.

She checked the reading on the Mach meter, an instrument that measures such high speeds.

"Mach .97," she said into the microphone so that Chuck could hear her. She was nearing Mach 1, the speed of sound.

"Mach .98."

The left wing suddenly dipped. Then the plane tilted wildly the other way and the right wing dipped. Then the nose began to act as if it wanted to turn the plane on its back.

"Mach .99," Jackie said quickly but with confidence.

The plane shook as the air began to build up like a wall in front of it. Jackie acted quickly to control its movements.

"Mach 1," she called out.

"Mach 1.01." She was through the dangerous sound, or sonic, barrier!

Inside the plane there was silence. At that speed, Jackie was flying so fast she was leaving the roar of the jet engine behind her.

She began now to pull gently out of the dive. Again the plane jerked wildly as she slowed it to below the speed of sound.

When Jackie landed and got out of the plane, friends at the air base rushed to congratulate her.

"I was so happy I felt like I was walking ten feet off the ground," she later told Floyd.

Before the plane was returned to Canada, Jackie set three world speed records and dived three times past the sonic barrier.

Messages poured in from people all over the world. Among them was a special letter of congratulations from her good friend President Eisenhower.

Later Jackie received the International Flying Organization's gold medal "for the outstanding accomplishment by any pilot, man or woman, during 1953."

In the years that followed, Jackie was often in poor health, but she continued to fly. Many more awards came her way, including the Legion of Merit and the Distinguished Flying Cross.

Helping other people, especially children, continued to take up much of her time. Her husband, too, seemed never too busy to reach out and help another person even though he was too sick to lead a very active life. In all of their years together, Jackie had learned that he was one of the kindest, gentlest, and most generous human beings she had ever known.

In 1953 Jackie was voted Business Woman of the Year. She enjoyed her business success, but it no longer seemed important to her. She sold her Jacqueline Cochran line of cosmetics several years later.

In 1954 Jackie wrote an exciting book about herself. The title was *The Stars at Noon.*

Seeing the stars at noon while teetering on the edge of space was only one of the many thrills that flying brought to her life. She once flew around the Taj Mahal in India by moonlight and circled around the crater Vesuvius in Italy.

She was the first woman to land a jet on an aircraft carrier; the first woman to fly to Mach 2, twice the speed of sound; the first woman to pilot a jet across the Atlantic.

In 1963 her tests of the military fighter plane, the F104G Starfighter, helped to clear up its reputation as a plane that was dangerous to fly.

Jackie and her F104G Starfighter. She had truly become the "first lady of flight."

Jackie's name and list of accomplishments now hangs in the Aviation Hall of Fame in Dayton, Ohio, along with those of other leaders in aviation.

At a banquet in 1971, Jackie was admitted to the Society of Experimental Test Pilots. When the society's president introduced her to the hundreds of test pilots present, he told them, "Jacqueline Cochran has done more for aviation than many of you men."

Loud applause burst through the hall.

It was a proud moment for Jackie. Even though she was no longer test flying, her heart and mind went out to those who still braved the dangers of the sky for the good of aviation.

"With my last breath," she said, "I'll be on the aerial sidelines cheering those who are carrying on."

Index

A

Alcott, Louisa May, 36, 37
American Foundation for the Blind, 109
Arnold, H. H. (Hap), 148, 152, 153
Aviation Hall of Fame, 164

B

Bancroft, Anne, 19
Bangs, Edward, 16–17, 19, 20, 22
Bell, Alexander Graham, 88 (pic), 89, 105 (pic)
Bellevue Hospital, 62, 63, 65 (pic), 66
Bendix Transcontinental Air Race, 140–142, 143, 146
Boston City Hospital, 55, 56, 72
Bowden, Helen, 63, 64, 66
Braille, 96, 97, 102, 106
Bridgeman, Laura, 88
Butler, Cyrus, 29, 30

C

Carlisle, Grafton, 149
Channing, William, 20, 22, 23, 27, 28
Child labor, 125, 126 (pic), 128
Civil War, 34, 35, 36, 37, 52
Cochran, Jacqueline, 117 (pic), 159 (pic)
  aids needy children, 162
  as author, 162
  as beauty operator, 127, 128, 129, 130, 132
  and Bendix Continental Air Race, 140, 141, 142, 143, 144 (pics), 145 (pics), 146
  breaks sound barrier, 160–161
  childhood of, 118, 119, 120, 121, 122, 123, 124
  and cosmetic business, 136, 137, 157, 162
  as director of Women's Air Force Service Pilots (WASP), 153, 154 (pic), 155, 156, 157
  education of, 121, 122, 123
  as ferry pilot, 148–149, 150
  and first air race, 137, 138, 139, 140
  as flier in England, 151 (pic), 152, 153
  as flight consultant, 158
  flying records of, 136–137, 161, 162
  honors and awards to, 161, 162, 164
  learns to fly, 134, 135, 136
  meets Floyd Odlum, 133
  as mill worker, 125, 126–127
  as nurse, 130, 131, 132
  as test pilot, 147, 148, 158, 162
Cochran-Odlum ranch, 147, 155
Conversations on Common Things (Dix), 22

D

Dimock, Susan, 57, 60, 62, 64
Dix, Charles (brother of Dorothea Dix), 11, 13, 14, 21
Dix, Dorothea Lynde, 9 (pic), 32 (pic)
  as author, 22
  birth of, 11
  childhood of, 10, 11, 12, 13, 14
  education of, 15
  fights for improved care of mentally ill, 27, 28, 29, 30, 31, 32, 33, 38
  visits England, 23–25, 33
  last years of, 39
  as schoolteacher, 19, 21, 22
  as superintendent of United States Army Nurses (Civil War), 35, 36, 37, 38
Dix, Elijah (grandfather of Dorothea Dix), 10, 11, 12, 13, 31
Dix, Joseph (father of Dorothea Dix), 10, 13
Dix, Joseph (brother of Dorothea Dix), 11, 12, 14, 21, 38
Duncan, Sarah, 12, 15

E

Eaton, Joseph, 19

Edwards Air Force Base, 158
Eisenhower, Dwight D., 161

F

Fiske, Sarah, 15, 16, 17, 19
Fuller, Sarah, 100

G

Gee Bee, 137, 138
Green, Lucy, 19

H

Heath, Ann, 20, 21, 22, 25, 31, 38
Helen Keller World Crusade, 114
Hospital Sketches (Alcott), 37
Howe, Samuel, 27, 28
Huckleberry Finn (Twain), 102

I

"If I Had Three Days to See" (Keller), 112
International Flying Organization, 161

K

Keller, Helen, 83 (pic), 105 (pic), 109 (pic)
  as author, 112
  birth of, 85
  childhood of, 84, 85, 86, 87, 88, 89, 94 (pic)
  goes to college, 103–104
  education of, 95, 96, 98, 99, 101, 103–104
  honors to, 113
  learns to communicate, 91–93, 100 (pic)
  as lecturer, 106, 108, 111
  appears in movie, 108
  at the Perkins Institute, 98, 99
  meets Anne Sullivan, 90
  travels in Europe, 113
  travels in Japan, 111
  works to aid blind and deaf, 106, 107, 109, 111, 112, 113, 114
Keller, Mildred (sister of Helen Keller), 84

L

Lighthouse for the Blind, 107
Lincoln, Abraham, 34, 52
Lincoln, Levi, 19
Lincoln, William, 19
Lip reading, 101
Little Women (Alcott), 36

M

Macy, Anne Sullivan. *See* Sullivan, Anne
Macy, John, 103, 104, 106, 107
Mann, Horace, 28
Massachusetts General Hospital, 66
Mentally ill, the
  hospital care of, 24, 80, 81
  improved care of, 28, 29, 38–39, 80
  treatment of, 24, 26–27, 28, 29 (pic), 80

N

National Library for the Blind, 106
New England Hospital for Women and Children, 57, 81
Nichols, John, 25, 26
Nightingale, Florence, 56, 64, 68, 69, 70 (pic), 71
Nightingale Training School, 67, 68
Nurses
  and care of patients, 64, 65–66
  during Civil War, 35, 36, 37 (pic), 54
  pensions for, 38
  prejudices against, 54, 60, 66, 72
  training of, 59–60, 61 (pic), 72, 73, 80
  training schools for, 58, 62, 66, 67, 71–72
  early uniforms of, 65

O

Odlum, Floyd B. (husband of Jacqueline Cochran), 133 (pic), 134, 135, 136, 140, 141, 143, 146, 147, 148, 152, 157, 161, 162

P

Perkins Institute, the, 88, 90, 98, 99
Poole, George, 51, 52

R

Radcliffe College, 103
Richards, Elizabeth (sister of Linda Richards), 43, 44, 45, 49
Richards, Laura (sister of Linda Richards), 43, 44, 45
Richards, Melinda Ann Judson (Linda), 41 (pic)
  at Bellevue Hospital, 62–65, 66
  birth of, 42
  childhood of, 42, 43, 44, 45, 46, 47, 48
  death of, 81
  and death of mother, 43–45
  as director of nurses at mental hospital, 80
  early nursing experiences, 44, 46, 47, 48
  education of, 50
  heads training program at Boston City Hospital, 72
  works in Japan, 73, 74, 75 (pic)
  at Massachusetts General Hospital, 66–67
  attends Nightingale Training School, 68, 70–71
  becomes nurse, 62
  teaches school, 50, 51, 52
  and Visiting Nurses Society, 76, 77, 79
  works as maid at Boston City Hospital, 55–56
  last years of, 81
Roosevelt, Franklin D., 112, 151

S

Sabre Jet F-86, 158, 159 (pic)
St. Elizabeth's Hospital, 34
St. Johnsbury Academy, 50
St. Thomas's Training School, 68, 69, 70
Seversky pursuit plane, 143, 144 (pic)
Smith, Wesley, 137, 138, 139, 140
Society of Experimental Test Pilots, 164
Starfighter F104G, 162, 163 (pic)
Stars at Noon, The (Cochran), 162
Stringer, Tommy, 99, 107, 112
Sullivan, Anne, 90, 91, 92, 93, 95, 96, 97, 99, 100 (pic), 101, 102, 103, 105 (pic), 106, 108, 110
Sumner, Charles, 27

T

Thompson, Polly, 107, 108, 111
Tom Sawyer (Twain), 101
Trenton State Hospital, 34, 39
Tuke, Samuel, 24
Twain, Mark, 101, 102

V

Visiting Nurses Society, 77, 78 (pic), 79

W

Wheeler, Frances, 16, 17, 19
Wheeler, Nancy, 16, 19
Women's Air Force Service Pilots (WASP), 153, 154 (pic), 155, 156, 157
World War I, 108
World War II, 112, 113, 148, 152, 157
Wright-Humason School, 101

Y

Yeager, Charles (Chuck), 158, 160
York Retreat, 24